Godwink

On The Wings of Butterflies

By Bridgette Hester
with Terri Lang

Godwink:
On the Wings of Butterflies
©2012, 2013 Bridgette Hester, with Terri Lang
All Rights Reserved

Second Edition

Cover Image Credit: Michael Vishkoff (aka) TMV3
Interior Tower Image Credit: Corey Johnson
Cover Design: Elizabeth E. Little, Hyliaan Graphics
Interior Formatting: Ellen Sallas, The Author's Mentor,
www.theauthorsmentor.com
Author Website: http://www.hubblefoundation.org/
Author Photo Credit: Wanda Tillman Williams

ISBN-13: 978-1491250891
ISBN-10: 1491250895
Also available in eBook

For The Father,
The Son,
The Holy Spirit,
& The Hunny Bunn

You turned my wailing into dancing;
You removed my sackcloth and clothed me with joy,
that my heart may sing Your praises and not be silent.
LORD my God, I will praise You forever.
~Psalm 30:11-12 *(NIV)*

ABLE OF CONTENTS

Imagery illustration courtesy of Sonya Crask. On this page, Sonya, your creation could not be more perfect. I love you!

PREFACE

    I will not claim that I know your loss, your experience, or your grief. What I *will* say is that I have traveled this road too. I *will* say that the experience is different, but the destination is the *same*—the realization that you matter, your pain matters, and your happiness and fulfillment matter to God. I am a work in progress. God loves me, but I can be boisterous, a little brash on occasion, and blunt. Despite all that, He *loves* me. He *loves* you. Therefore, while I do not expect my story to "fix" anything or to "counsel" anyone, it is intended to be a modicum of comfort to women or men in this world who have experienced the loss of a husband or wife. I will guide you through areas of my life with my husband that were good, bad, and indifferent. In the end, the message I want you to come away with is that we are human; we mess up, grieve, beat ourselves up, and block ourselves from His grace (don't let yourself do that). God is there; lean on Him, let Him absorb it for you, let Him in, and accept His grace. If you do, the journey is one that ends in peace and ultimately happiness.

"Come to Me, all you who labor and are heavy laden, and I will give you rest."
Matthew 11:28 (NKJV)

**You will see many Scriptures written out and some Scriptures referenced by book, chapter, and verse only. I encourage you to read them, look them up, and explore them.

ACKNOWLEDGEMENTS

Terri Lang is a dear friend of mine in my Wednesday night bible study. Terri recounted a story of her eldest daughter, Tessa and her, discussing how recent earthquakes are the birth pains of the earth, signifying that Jesus' return is near *(Matthew. 24:7,8 (NIV)*. Her youngest daughter, Erica, having overheard this conversation, ran around the room excited and proclaiming "Jesus is coming back soon, and we get to see him!" This precious child, just days later, was viciously accosted by two little red fire ants on her finger, to which she said, "I wish they [Adam and Eve] had never bitten that apple." Humorous as the story was in the family of my bible group, it wasn't until days later that I realized that this child, at a tender age of five, had captured the feeling I had inside me just a year and a half earlier when my husband, Jonce was killed. I had never been able to articulate the sense of loss, pain, and grief from losing him, until I heard the fire ant story.

How incredible is the unquestioning belief, faith, and commitment of a child to her Creator. There was no hesitation, no doubt, just indisputable fact. These two little fire ants had accosted her finger simply because Adam and Eve had disobeyed God's command not to eat from the Tree of Knowledge *(Gen. 3:6 (NKJ)*.

I have news for you. Despite what you have been taught, think to be true, or what wanton cultural legends may imply, this world is not what God intended for His children. The bad, ugly, nasty circumstances and happenings of this world are not a result of His lack of intervention, His disdain for His children, or an apathetic attitude by the Creator. The events that can (and do) happen to people are a direct result of the disobedience of God's first two human creations, and often because of their own sin. We all allow ourselves to wander out from under the umbrella of God's authority.

After hearing Erica's proclamation, I laughed and thought that it was the most precious thing I had heard in quite a while. Up to this point, since the death of my husband, I had come to several conclusions. I had recognized, in fact, that He was present, always had been, I just was not as aware of him as I should have been; my heart had been closed. Another conclusion I had come to was that God did not fail me. He in fact *prepared* me for the death of my husband. I also became acutely aware after Jonce's death, that, despite what I might have believed until that point, I was not in control. I was not in control of my life, my finances, my job, my marriage, my education, my friends…my anything; He was. I was just too consumed with the things of this world and myself to accept that fact.

Now, when this revelation hit me, I accepted it as fact and moved on. "Yep, You are the one in control not me. Got it. Check." However, the more I pondered on this reality, the more I realized the gravity of this admission, and I was completely shocked by what followed. Peace.

He controls all of it, not me. For a control freak, type "A" personality, this realization can feel a bit weighty. What I was not expecting was the indescribable relief that came, the unmitigated joy, the profound sense of release and comfort. Granted, this was not an overnight event. It is not to say my husband died, and the next day I was peaceful, far from it. The range of emotions after the death of your spouse is simultaneous and conflicting at times. On many levels those feelings are, incomprehensible to the human mind. This process gradually took me where He wanted me to go - a place He knew I needed to be. I am not always articulate, but I have had a journey, and continue to have one. I am not always pleasant, or understanding. I still get angry and confused. I am human, but God's not done with me yet. I hope you will read the entire process within these pages. Maybe you will recognize a little of yourself in here. I hope you recognize the "you" that you used to be, and the "you" that God wants you to become. Millions of people lose their spouse. Some may have had a similar experience to what I will describe here, but for others the journey is different.

"I am leaving you with a gift-peace of mind and heart. And the peace I give is a gift the world cannot give. So don't be troubled or afraid"
John 14:27 (NLT)

For the word of God is living and active, sharper than any two-edged sword, piercing to the division of soul and of spirit, of joints and of marrow, and discerning the thoughts and intentions of the heart.
Hebrews 4:12 (ESV)

 # WORD FROM TERRI LANG

From the moment Bridgette first mentioned God was leading her to write this book, I heard in my spirit, "she is 'A voice in the wilderness preparing the way of the Lord.'" (Malachi 3:1 & Matthew 3:3). This was the beginning of a journey of blessings and new beginnings for each of us.

It has truly been an honor to serve the Lord and you, Bridgette, through *Godwink: On the Wings of Butterflies.* I feel tremendously blessed by witnessing God's grace working through you. I have grown so much through this process, and it has prepared me to receive from the Lord; I might have missed what He has had in store for me if I had not been ready to receive you into my life. You have taught me a new level of trust, love and the value of friendship.

I thank you, Bridgette, for allowing me to "fly" with you on the wings of your butterflies. I love you, my sister, and friend. I also Praise God for my mentors, Ken and Gladys Hodge. Without them teaching me how to listen for God's voice and receive His love, I would still be lost. I am forever grateful. May God be given all the glory. I also want to thank my dear friend Renee` Rogers, who reminded me to expect God's goodness (let the frogs be gone today!) I love you.

❧❧

Have you ever wondered what a butterfly would be like in human form? Butterflies are tiny creatures whose flight patterns are fast, busy, and sometimes a little dizzying. However, they are relentless in achieving their goals. When they come near, their delicate wings and kaleidoscope of colors awe us. Butterflies give joy and peace when they rest upon something or someone.

Now take a moment and put a name to the image that just entered your mind. That name would be Bridgette Hester. A smile is brought immediately to my face and heart whenever she comes to mind. Bridgette is without a doubt a butterfly! Full of God's glory, grace, adventure, and anticipation, this little butterfly is ready! Bridgette is ready to receive and give God's goodness to all He puts in her path, and at times, she is almost anxious with all the energy the Lord has given her. After all, she has many places to go and so many people to bless.

The beauty of God's spirit resting and caring for Bridgette humbles me. I have watched in wonder as God has loosed this butterfly from her cocoon, to see her emerge victorious and free. Each of us, that includes you, is God's creation. At times, we are butterflies, flowers, and sometimes seeds. Our lives flow and exist in seasons. Some seasons are waiting for a beginning, some are receiving a beginning, and others are giving a beginning to others. With Jesus, old things are passed away (2 Cor. 5:17). What we need to remember is that each season is new, and that it did not come to stay, for all seasons pass. Each season carries us to where we need to be, to grow us into who we are supposed to be, and to usher in the new. (I encourage you to read Ecclesiastes 3:1-8).

During our lives, as we live out our seasons, God is who carries us to and through and we need to be ready to follow the wind of the Holy Spirit. Be ready to receive what He has for us. Sometimes that will push us out of our cocoon, our comfort zone. If we resist the change, we may miss the Lord revealing His glory. Romans 8:14, 18-22, tells us how all of creation groans and awaits eagerly for His glory to be revealed in the sons of God. That is us! We are both the creation and the sons and daughters of God, and we are groaning, waiting for His glory to be revealed and to receive our liberty. If we allow God to guide us, we can rest assured that He has already given us everything we need to overcome the circumstances. We will be able to emerge from cocoons of isolation, despair, and pain. He gave us Jesus! If we are ready to trust Jesus and receive His presence, we too will emerge victorious and free.

8

"For whom the Son sets free are free indeed" (John 8:36) (*paraphrase mine*) Are you ready? Are you ready to receive the abundant life God has promised you? If so, look to Jesus. Ask Him in your heart, stay in His Word, and learn His voice (John 10:27). God promised to never leave you, to never forsake you (Deut. 31:6). He will send you your Godwink along the way. God bless you little butterflies!

May God's peace, love, and blessings be on each one of you all the days of your lives! Be Ready!
Love, Terri Lang

PART ONE

JULY 22, 2010

1

$\mathcal{T}$IL DEATH DO US PART...

My paternal grandmother died in 1989 from breast cancer. My mom died in 2003 from colon cancer, and *her* mother, my maternal grandmother, died ten days before my mother from a heart condition. Then I lost a friend from HIV in 2007, my natural father in 2008 from lung cancer, and a few others along the way from accidents or illness. In addition, there have been countless numbers of funerals and viewings of friends, friends of friends, and relatives of friends of friends … You get the picture. However, the death of my husband, was the most personally tragic and painful experience with death I have ever encountered. I will never forget those two missed phone calls and that one fateful text message.

I had been awake for practically the entire three days prior to that Thursday. My caseload at work included a woman and man who had absconded with their children as they were coming into foster care due to neglect and abuse. They ran on Monday night, and by Wednesday, the children had been located in Mississippi, so another worker and I were en route to retrieve the children. I got back home around midnight on Thursday, July 22, 2010. I had just laid my head on the pillow when the phone rang. One of the children I had dropped off to a safe foster family apparently had blood in her diaper.

I lightly kissed Jonce, who had just settled in for the night, and told him I had to head thirty miles back down the road.

"What? You just got home. What the——?"

"I know baby, but I have to check on this kid. If she's bleeding in her diaper, there's no telling what happened to her while she was with her parents. I have to go."

"Fine. I will just see you in the morning."

Jonce kissed me and proceeded to roll over in the covers and burrow in until I returned. I gave him another peck and a loud "I love you!" As the door closed, I heard, "I love you too, baby."

Three hours later, I dragged myself home, crawled into bed, and kissed Jonce on the cheek and snuggled up, close as two spoons in a drawer. Come six in the morning, like clockwork, Jonce got up and dressed and bee lined out the door at six-thirty to get to work on time. I was never thrilled about Jonce's job. Jonce was a telecommunications worker, otherwise referred to as a "tower climber" or "tower dog." Jonce and his tower crew installed, performed maintenance on, and sometimes erected telecommunications towers around the country. Often tower dogs climb hundreds or thousands of feet in the air, held to a tower by a harness and fall protection equipment. It has been reported to be the most dangerous job in the U.S., and it is not a job for the faint of heart.

When he left that morning, I *know* he kissed me, I *know* he told me he loved me. He did so *every day, without fail.* I only vaguely recall this, as I had barely been asleep for three hours and have no real recollection of him getting up from bed. I think, I recall a garbled "I love you too" from my lips as he headed out the door. I can't swear to it, but I know he used to make fun of me for my unintelligible responses to this morning ritual when I was too exhausted to wake up as he left.

I got up around seven thirty and proceeded to prepare for a court hearing on the children we picked up in Mississippi. I went to the court hearing, and made sure the children were allocated to a safe foster home. I then asked my boss for a half day to rest after having been up all night. On the drive back to the house at ten fifty-three a.m., as I crossed the causeway over the lake, I called Jonce to tell him I was headed home. I told him that if he needed me, I would be home asleep but would leave my phone on. It was during this call when I realized he was on a tower.

"Errruuughhhh! #^%*$%!"

"What, what's wrong?"

"This tower is a nightmare, I can't... never mind, baby; it's just work. Dang thing won't cooperate. Go home and get some sleep. You have been up too long and you need to rest. I will see you tonight when I get home."

"I really wish you wouldn't answer the phone on the tower. It gives me the jeebers. Just be careful. I love you."

"Oh my God! What—? Okay, okay, okay, I love you. I gotta go. This thing is driving me nuts. Love you."

"Love you too. Bye, baby."

I look back on this exchange now (and this is the closest I remember the conversation verbatim, though I may have missed something or a sentiment, for everything is still fuzzy for me, even now) and realize this was the last exchange I had with Jonce. *Sigh.* We told each other we loved one another—I hold that dear. Priceless. Invaluable. A person should never hang up the phone or leave the house without saying those words, for you never know if it will be the last time you get to tell them or hear those words spoken to you.

I continued home, fell into bed, and was out like a light. Murphy's Law tends to reign in my life. I had only been out for about an hour. The phone rang twice, and I didn't answer it because I did not recognize the number. I needed sleep. Unless it was Jonce, I wasn't answering the phone. No more than a couple minutes later, I received a text message from the same number. "Call me now. Jonce has been in an accident!"

There is no description of the fear and adrenaline that pulsed through me. For a tower dog's wife to get a message like that... well, let's just say it couldn't be good. He had a minor mishap or two on other jobs (a broken finger, a hurt knee), but I generally learned about this after the fact. I found out when I called the number that it was Tim McCord, his boss. Apparently, a truck had backed into the guyed wires (structure support wires) and the tower fell. Jonce had been on the tower with his co-worker, Barry Sloan, about thirty to forty feet up when the tower collapsed. Jonce's leg and arm were "messed up" and he had lost some blood, but they were taking him to the hospital.

I ran around the house gathering my purse and keys, flying out the door while on the phone.

"Okay, his arm and his leg? Seriously? How bad? Broken? Dislocated?"

Silence.

"Dang it, Tim. How bad?"

"Honey, just come on. They are probably going to be able to fix him up; just come."

"Tim ..."

"It looks like hamburger meat. He needs you. Get a ride and meet us at the hospital."

"Keep me updated. I am leaving now."

"You're driving? I don't think that's a good idea."

"Yeah, well, we can argue about that later. Call me and keep me updated."

I bolted out the door and called several friends and family on the way. I was chastised numerous times for driving myself in my upset condition, but I was not about to wait twenty minutes for someone to get me. No way. No how. I called Jonce's stepmother, Martha, and explained the situation but asked her to keep quiet to Jonce's daughter, Becky for the moment, until I knew what we were dealing with. She agreed.

I slammed the phone down in the passenger seat and ratcheted up my speed. I made countless other calls to friends, Jonce's brothers, and Alison Sloan. Oddly, I was the reason that Alison's husband, Barry, was working for McCord. Alison had interned with us at the department of human resources and she helped me one night on a foster care case. We talked, and when I found out her husband was a tower dog looking to get back in the field, I mentioned Jonce and told her to have Barry go to McCord's and fill out the application. Alison and I knew Barry got the job before Barry did. We giggled about it then. I wasn't giggling anymore.

I called Alison and told her that there had been an accident. I told her not to freak out and that I was still getting information. I told her to try to get a hold of Tim. She told me she was on her way home and that there was someone there waiting for her. I told her I loved her and that we would talk later. She agreed, and the phone call ended. Immediately after this call, I got another from Tim stating they were leaving the local hospital and Jonce was being life-flighted to University of Alabama's Hospital in Birmingham.

"I'm sorry? What the ...? Life flighted? Tim, talk to me."

"Do you know where it is?"

"I'll find it, why the life flight? We had a messed up arm and leg! You are scaring me Tim, what... come on!!!!"

"Just get there. My dad (Mike McCord, the Co-owner of the company) will be there to meet you, go through the ER. Every one of us is on the way after the police and medics clear out."

"What about Barry?"

Again, there was silence.

"Tim...What about Barry?"

"Barry's gone, honey, he died on scene."

I then ended the call to digest what Tim had told me. While I was pondering what to tell Alison, the phone rang.... Alison. Oh, Lord. Does she know? She could not have spoken to Tim; I just hung up with him. Oh God, I won't be able to keep my mouth shut. She's driving. I cannot, I will not, give her this kind of news over the phone. Cowardly, as it may have been, I refused to answer. How do you tell your friend that her husband's dead? I couldn't have that conversation right now, at least not in the manner it deserved. I decided to give Tim a little more time to get her on the phone. I just prayed she didn't have cops sitting in the drive when she got home.

I then called our friends Misty and Steve and all but barked orders at them to give me directions to UAB while I was en route. Three or four wrong exits later, hysterical and beating the tear soaked steering wheel, I found myself off the interstate and completely confused about where the ER was located. I did the only rational thing I could do right then. I pulled up to a parking garage as nurses appeared crossing the entrance. I parked the car got out and yelled and literally kidnapped the nearest nurse I could find.

"Hey, HEYYYY!!!! SIR!!! My husband has been in a horrific work accident, I can't find the ER, I need you to--- God PLEASE--- get in my car. Take me there! NOW! PLEASE!"

He was a slender male, with kind eyes. I wish I could remember his name. Bless this man's soul. He never missed a beat, never looked taken aback, and never questioned me. Angels exist on earth. I promise you. Some of the most amazing ones dress in scrubs.

As he walked to the passenger door and belted himself in, he calmly instructed me to the ER entrance. During the short ride, I thanked him repeatedly and explained what little I knew. He said he would say a prayer for this man, my husband, a man he had never met. I thanked him and once I pulled into the garage, he departed, and I bolted around the garage deck and through the front door. Then I waited. Ten minutes I waited, frantically, wringing my hands. However, through these ten minutes, I had Mike McCord at my side. He told me they had already taken Jonce back to surgery for his arm and leg. He explained what he knew of the accident, but I was only half listening. I wanted the nurse, I wanted attention, and I wanted to see my husband. Once the nurse finally got to me, she stated that Jonce was in surgery, and that I needed to sit in the waiting room and that someone would come get me. I relented, unhappily, and sat in the chairs as instructed.

Mike stated others were on their way, but it could be a while. Jonce and Barry had been on the tower and attaching co-ax cable to the tower. The job was completed. The third party company, that operated the crane, had left the site and things were fine. He stated the third party came back up the hill with a thirty-three-foot bucket truck to retrieve the tractor-trailer. Mike said he did not know all of the details, but as the bucket truck was turning around, he clipped the guyed wires, which stabilize the tower. The tower fell and Barry died on site when the base of the tower fell on him, and that Jonce had been attached further up (as safety guidelines instruct). He stated that when the tower fell with Jonce connected to it, it collapsed and buried Jonce in some of the debris.

At this point, a thousand questions screamed through my mind, but asking them, right then was of little importance. I would deal with those once Jonce was out of surgery and we had time to talk. I needed to find out what kind of rehabilitation we were looking at and what kind of additional medical care might be needed. The phrases "hamburger meat" "probably going to be able to fix him up" wouldn't leave me alone. It was during this time I also made additional calls to Jonce's father, Andray, and Jonce's brother and sister-in-law, Jason and B.J. I found out that Andray would arrive in a matter of minutes, Martha, his wife (Jonce's stepmother) had Jonce's children (my stepchildren) Becky, Daniel, and Michael, and they too were en route. Shane and Joey, Jonce's stepbrothers, were on the way, as were Jason and B.J. So. I waited.

I was then called back into a private family "waiting area." "Oh, this does not feel like this is going to end well," I thought. I could feel it, but I kept myself in check. Mike sat with me, held my hands, and kept telling me that he was so sorry and whatever I needed he would provide. With a grim smile, I told him, "You already are." I hugged him fiercely and allowed myself a few tears. Jonce's work crew, the office staff, and Tim and Mike, are family, they are not just co-workers. Breaking down at that moment however was not much of an option, because one of the medical staff walked in.

She told me Jonce was out of surgery and on the way to some other test. She stated there appeared to be fluid on his abdomen and they needed the test to see to what extent. She stated the trauma surgeon would be in to see me in a moment, and that when Jonce was brought back up, I would be able to see him. I asked for some water and left the room. I went back to the waiting room because I felt like I couldn't breathe in that small room. All I wanted was Jason and B.J. It was then I ran into Andray, Jason, and B.J. as they walked through the emergency room doors. We all embraced, and I filled them in on what I knew and then led them back to the private waiting area.

It wasn't long before Dr. Melton, the lead trauma surgeon, arrived. According to her, Jonce fell from the tower and had been covered in debris, which had caused serious life threatening injuries. She stated emergency surgery had to be preformed in order to save his life. I don't remember much of the actual words from this point on, until she said the word "amputation." Suffocated by the event, I wasn't processing information too well, and I had her repeat her last words.

"Due to the severity of his injuries, in order to save his life, his left arm above the elbow (not quite to the shoulder), and his right leg above the knee needed to be amputated."

"Huh. I'm sorry, come again?"

"I know this is a great deal of information to take in Mrs. Hubble, and I am so sorry. However, right now, we need to take him back to surgery to remove some fluid that has built up ..."

I know I agreed to the surgery, but there is a point when your brain will tune out the details once you have the basic premise of what is before you. I turned to her before she left and asked about his ring. She smiled and pulled it from her pocket. A ring. His ring. A beautiful white gold ring in a tiny little plastic bag. I thanked her as I took it from her hand. I looked back to her after I had gotten it out.

"Oh. Um, do you have something?... I need... *Sigh.* There's blood on this and I need to clean it. Right Now."

"I was going to do that for you, but getting to you was my priority. Come with me, and let's have someone get that cleaned for you. I am going to get Jonce from the test, and you and the family can come see him before we take him in for the additional surgery."

My sister-in-law, B.J., never left my side. I grabbed her when I my eyes found her again and I did my best to keep her near me. I always refer to her as "MY B.J." and I didn't want her to lose sight of me. She is a character to say the least. She is bold, lovingly abrasive, and she will tell you like it is. I love and adore her, I always will. I had a feeling that I was going to need some brutal honesty before too long, and no one I knew was better at that than B.J. She walked with Dr. Melton and me, and stayed with me while they cleaned the ring. We walked back to the waiting room until we were able to go see Jonce.

At some point, Jonce's mother, Connie, had arrived. I have absolutely no recollection of what I said to her. The conversations I had with family and doctors are an approximation of my memory and what family have told me was said. I never really believed it, but trauma has a way of warping time and memory. Sometimes everything is grainy, fuzzy, and just so blurry I can't remember clearly. This day especially can be clear as a mud hole. Other days, sights and sounds trigger memories of this day as clear as a bell and sharp as a tack.

Dr. Melton came in, shortly after I returned from having Jonce's ring cleaned. It was probably more like a couple of hours. When she came back in, she tried to prepare us for what we would see, and then led Andray, Connie, Jason, and me back to see Jonce. I don't know if no one else could come, or if B.J. just chose to stay in the family waiting room. Dr. Melton told us he was unconscious and heavily sedated and wouldn't be able to speak. She stated that we had a minimal amount of time because she needed to get him into surgery for his abdominal injuries.

I twirled Jonce's ring around my finger and marched down the hall to see Jonce, kiss his face, and reassure him everything was going to be fine. This was just a little hiccup; we were going to get through this. Period. I mean, for crying out loud, we hadn't been married a full four years yet. He was going to be *fine*. A hiccup, just a hiccup. Then there is that moment when you *know* something. You just *know*, there is no mistaking it, there's no getting away from it, you *know* that you *know*. *It's not going to be "OK."* That moment hit me the second I looked at Jonce.

We gathered around a cold steel table, it wasn't even a bed. His eyes were closed, he was unconscious, and there would be no conversation. At least not a two-way conversation. I think I went first. I bent down next to his left ear, and I told him...

"You better get on with it already Hunny Bunn, this is not the time. You are the most stubborn man I have ever met. When you get into that OR, you had better *fight*. You had better *fight* like you never have. If you don't, I will personally kick your butt. Look Jonce, bionic limbs. Surely, they make them. One arm and one leg? We can totally handle this. I'll even make sure your prostheses are decorated for Alabama Football. Just get in there and *fight*. I love you *so* much, so so much."

I gently bent down and kissed him where I could on his face, scared I was going to injure him further. Despite the gravity of the situation, when I looked up, the nursing team gave me small smiles. At first I thought maybe they thought it was cute the way I was egging him on, but I later realized, those small smiles were smiles of "Oh, Lord, Bless her heart, please be with her." Then there was that one moment, where I let myself think, "Jonce is not here. @#$^%&$^%. Jonce isn't here."

Guilt and fear immediately hit me and I inwardly made myself regroup. I kept telling myself there was no room for that, and I then started the silent prayers for him to live. I didn't care at that moment how hard it would be, how incredibly angry he would be, how pained he would be at my having to take care of him. I didn't care. I just wanted him to wake up, to get better, and to come back to me.

While his mom, dad, and brother bent and kissed him and said their own versions of love and encouragement, I spoke with Dr. Melton.

"I am going to take him to surgery, and we are going to remove the fluid from his abdomen. The amount of trauma that he has sustained is *massive*. I am going to do *everything* that I can to save his life."

"I don't care what you have to do. Just do it."

"You know that I will. I just need you to be prepared that…. I am going to do everything that I can possibly do to save him, but …"

"Bbbuuutt…"

"I am going to do everything Mrs. Hubble, but I am not hopeful…"

"Hopeful or not, please take him in there, and work like you have never worked on another person, you try everything, you fix him, please fix him. Please."

Then, in a move I wouldn't have expected from the lead trauma surgeon, she folded me in a hug and stroked my back. When she whispered to me again that she would do everything she could, I knew she was telling me the truth. However, I also felt another truth creeping back in…. He's not here for her to save.

◈◈

When I pulled back, I saw it right in her eyes, and I think that was the first real moment I accepted it, at least quietly to myself. I was quick to try to shake it off, and we all headed back down the hall. I don't think anyone else heard her when she said those words to me. I walked back down the hall and grabbed B.J., and the floodgates opened. I sobbed, inwardly screamed, and then I pulled myself together again. Andray, Connie, B.J., Jason, and I then gathered to sit and pray in the family room. We then went to see the children and the rest of the family that had shown up by this point.

We all met in a small family room off the main ER lobby. Everyone looked so deflated, and this little talk wasn't going to help much. To be frank, I have absolutely no recollection of what I said. I believe in my heart of hearts that I told everyone gathered of his condition, and that he was on his way to another surgery. I do not recall if I mentioned the amputations of his limbs or not. I told the kids that we would wait and see where things stood after the surgery, but I am almost certain that I explained the severity of his injuries.

The children just sat. They listened, and I know that they heard me, but the blank looks that I got indicated that they knew what was coming. Daniel said nothing, Michael and Brad looked angry and sad, and Becky just looked completely mortified. We all did. I said the words, I tried to make things clear, and I attempted not to make things too scary, but honesty was important too. Telling four children how injured their dad is, without implying outright you think he is going to die, is not a discussion I wish on anyone. I wanted more in that moment than at any time in my life to be able to comfort them, bear their pain, make Jonce healthy again. There is nothing that made me feel more frustrated and helpless than to sit and watch the children retreat inwardly.

After the discussion with the family, I told them I would be out front of the ER if they needed me. I needed some air, some space, and most of all I needed my daddy. B.J. hugged me and squeezed my hand as I slipped out the door with tears threatening to spill over. The pressure building in me was unlike anything I had ever felt. My head was hurting, my tears were threatening to overflow, and I was ready to break into full hysterics. I wanted my daddy. I needed my daddy. Daddy would make it better; he could fix this. He would tell me that it was going to be fine. I knew I would believe him; I just needed him to say the words to reignite my faith, my stability, and my control. I hadn't even called him yet. How do I tell him this? How do I start? How do I even think of explaining this when I couldn't even wrap my own brain around it?

The time between leaving that room and hitting the front door of the ER, to walking past the sloped incline, and sitting on the stone wall by the street took maybe fifteen seconds. It felt like fifteen years. I dialed and as it was ringing, all I could think was that daddy wasn't answering me fast enough. Daddy, ppplllleeeaaassseeee pick u--.

"Daddy, oh my God, daddy."
"Baby girl, what is it, what's wrong?"
"DAAADDDDDYYYY... DDDAAA
DDDDDYYYYY!!!!!!!!!!!!!..."

Of the conversation, this is the only exchange I remember clearly. In a rush of words, I rambled, I tried to explain, and then the sound that rang forth from me was that of some suffering and injured animal. It wasn't words, it was just a sound. The only other time I made a sound, even remotely close to it, was the very second in which my mother took her last breath while I held her hand.

I retched and clutched the stone wall out in front of the ER. In my next clear memory of the call, I was screaming "Daddy!" repeatedly while I wailed against the wall. I remember my dad putting my stepmother on the phone. She seemed to be aware of what was going on and dad must have held the phone for her to hear me cry and scream uncontrollably.

What was my poor stepmother supposed to say? Bless her heart, she wanted to hold me, and take it from me, it felt as if she were trying to pull me through the phone so she could comfort me. Their hearts were breaking for me and I couldn't get to them, or they to me. This part of the call lasted three minutes, maybe less. Suddenly daddy was back on the line.

"Bridgette... Bridgette... baby girl, Listen to daddy."

"Ohhhhhh GOOOODDDDDD, Dddaddddyyy!!!, Amputated, surgery, Dddaaddddyyyy!!!!, Daddy help me!!!!"

"Baby girl, you listen to your daddy. When he gets out of surgery, you go in his room, and you hit your knees, baby. You hit your knees, and you pray. You pray and you don't stop. Hit your knees, baby."

"Ok, Ok, I swear daddy, I will, I promise."

Then the wailing came again. How long this lasted I am not sure, but it couldn't have been long. I only vaguely recall the conversation ending and my promising to call daddy again with more news.

I look back now on this and I can only imagine my father's pain during this call. My mom, had passed away exactly seven years and two days prior to my calling him on this day. The pain of losing a spouse is the most wrenching pain I have ever experienced. Even so, I can't *imagine* hearing your child wailing into the phone when he or she is experiencing the beginnings of what you know to be one of the worst losses of their life and being completely helpless to do anything about it.

Instinctively, parents want to protect and to shield their children from loss, pain, and grief. There are just no words for how he must have felt in that moment. My dad is the most amazing, loving, Godly man I know. I could feel him radiating love and prayers over the phone, but I could also feel his frustration at not being able to stop my fear or pain.

I didn't realize it then, and realized it only after Jonce's funeral when I spoke to my dad, but he had been in the middle of Biker Church when I called him. In addition to my parents, I had had ninety-five bikers on their knees praying for my husband, the family, and me. I may not have *known* that then, but I *felt* it, because I had felt it before. I felt it when they prayed for my mom seven years earlier.

My father is the pastor for "Redeemed Biker Church" in Hampton, Georgia. His congregation is bikers that don't readily feel welcome in your regular religious establishments. The average person's vision of a "biker" brings to mind, sex, drugs, rock and roll, tattoos, and the like. This is hardly a group that most Southern denominations would expect to stroll through the door Sunday morning.

Not all churches or their members would be unwelcoming to such a demographic I know, but most bikers just don't feel like they "fit in" at a regular church… thus, Biker Church. I totally and unequivocally LOVE daddy's congregation. OK, I am a biker, so I am a biased, but still. Bikers are fabulous people; fun, interesting, loving, and family oriented. Bikers are some of the most devoted and loyal friends I have ever had. They were there when my mom passed. They took care of daddy, my sister, her family, and me. They never wavered; they just loved us through it.

After the call to Daddy, I hung up, took a few minutes to straighten myself up, turned on my heel, and marched back to the ER. Most everyone was filing outside to smoke, or get some air, or to wander around; the activities of the lost and helplessly aimless. I think it may have been an hour or two before the nurse came to get our group. We rounded everyone up, and trekked to the ICU floor of the hospital. At this point, there is a train of some forty or more people following the family and me to the elevators. A wall of Jonce's co-workers, our friends, and extended family conversed quietly and filled the waiting area for news.

The time in ICU is still a blur to me, even today. I **think** I got to the hospital shortly after the noon hour. At this point, it was somewhere around two or three o'clock in the afternoon. Waiting room chairs were full and people were comforting one another, talking about the accident, crying, and praying. The immediate family and I were in a small conference room/meeting room/family area just inside ICU doors and meeting with Dr. Melton and the charge nurse.

A litany of information ensued. I got snippets of information as my mind floated back and forth between the urgency of the information, and completely random and irrelevant thoughts.

"His injuries are *past* critical. Jonce is losing blood and medication as fast as we are pumping them in."

Crud. Did feed the cats before I left?

"The surgery went as well as they could have expected given the blunt force trauma."

I think I will make steaks for Jonce for dinner, he likes steak.

"The outlook is not good, but we will do whatever you instruct us to do."

All of a sudden, I was snapped from wandering and I noticed it was quiet, and the doctor is looking at me.

"Mrs. Hubble…"

I conferred with Andray, Connie, Jason, and other family members with no words, just a look, or two. Andray started asking questions and seemed frustrated because either he didn't understand what they were telling him, was afraid, or he thought the staff wasn't doing enough. I would hazard it was all of the above. I just looked at the doctor. "Do it, give him whatever you need to give him, do whatever you need to do, you still do everything. I mean everything you can." The doctor agreed and agreed that two to four people, but no more, may visit with Jonce, while the team continued to work on him.

I (think) went alone first in to see Jonce. There were tubes everywhere, machines lit up, beeping at regular intervals, bags of blood and fluid on portable hooks around the bed. My first thought was how handsome he was. He, despite the environment, looked strong and peaceful and he did not appear to be in any pain. I think I may have only told a few people what I will confess now. When I walked in that ICU room, I knew he was gone. There was no tremble in his body, no flinch of movement, no anything, just peace. There was only unnerving quiet in-between signals on the pumps and machines. He was not present. Physically yes, but spiritually speaking, my husband had already left to go Home. I was looking at only a shell, his vessel.

On some level, I think I almost expected this. From the earlier conversation with Dr. Melton, my own desperation, the phone call with Daddy, facial expressions on the faces of his brothers, his kids, Jonce's father, and B.J. earlier in the day, and not one utterance of the reassuring words, just reinforced what had been foreshadowed earlier in my discussion with Dr. Melton. I had promised my daddy I would hit my knees to pray the minute I went into the room. Somehow, my knees wouldn't fold and the idea of praying never entered my mind. I struggled a long time with guilt over this after Jonce passed away, but when you see your husband lying on a table and you realize he isn't there, what would you really be praying for?

I approached the bed tentatively, slowly, afraid I might hurt him if I touched him, and afraid that I might break myself. I asked the trauma team if I could actually lay my hands on him, and they stated I could. I bent over and whispered in his ear that I loved him, that he needed to get better, and that I wanted and needed him to open his eyes. I shuddered and asked the charge nurse what they were doing. Beyond pushing platelets, blood, fluids, and medicine, there was not much else to do but watch vitals and check for brain stem activity. I leaned into him and kissed him again. I told him that his whole family was coming to see him and that I was conflicted about letting the kids see him in this state. I then told him I was probably going to allow it (after I talked to his dad), and if he had a problem with that, he would just have to sit up and chew me a new one. Nothing. No response.

I fought back more tears, sighed again, and waved a few people into the room. The only thing about the visits in the ICU that is fresh in my mind is the moment his brothers, Joey and Shane, walked in the room and when the kids came in to see Jonce. Joey and Shane's faces just crumpled with small almost undetectable utterances of "no... no... no" escaping their lips. Before allowing the children in the room, I talked with Andray, and he thought that it would hurt the kids more by not letting them see Jonce. Ultimately, I decided he was right, and I wasn't fighting anyone. I wanted the kids to remember their dad, just not like this. In the end though, I thank God every day that they were able to tell their dad goodbye.

The kids' breath caught in their throats and a look shown on all four faces of horror and fear combined. I watched the three boys do this "Hubble thing" where they become stoic faced with blank eyes. Jonce had a penchant for that look when he was hurting, not wanting anyone to know it. Becky just cried and cried; that completely broke

27

my heart.

After everyone had drifted in and out, to see Jonce, I spent about two hours moving from Jonce's room, to the family room, and to the waiting area to thank people for coming. Curiously, the waiting room was particularly depressing, yet hopeful at the same time. There was a sea of tear-stained faces, creased brows, and whispers of curiosity about the well-being of not only Jonce, but us, his family.

Pity, concern, and love radiated from the room every time I walked through. People hugged me, stroked my hair, my arm, and asked if I needed anything. I felt like a caged lion within the confines of the hospital. I kept waiting for someone in that waiting room to open my gate and let me out. Eventually as I walked through the last two or three times to go downstairs to get some fresh air, people just lowered their heads as I passed and didn't speak.

⊰⊱

Dr. Melton had come into the family room practically every hour on the hour with updates that became increasingly grim. I knew that a decision was coming. I did not want to make the decision I saw looming in my immediate future. I think the only ones present were the adults. I am almost completely positive I sent Becky out, and maybe Daniel. I distinctly remember that Michael and Brad refused to leave. The remainders of those in the family room with Dr. Melton were the charge nurse, his brothers, parents, B.J., and me. Through the next twenty minutes, Andray and I became agitated and demanded detailed explanations. We all knew it came from fear of what was coming and that we just wanted Jonce fixed. The patience of the staff was incomprehensible. At some point, I really just wanted to scream, but I knew the arguments and explanations were our way of delaying what we knew to be inevitable.

"Mrs. Hubble. We have done all we can do. We are pushing medication, fluids, and blood, but they are coming out as fast as we are able to pump them in. We are at a point where we checked for activity again. I am so sorry, but Jonce has no brain stem activity, and his eyes are fixed and dilated."

I heard only the roar of blood rushing through my own veins, although I am certain there were gasps, throat catches, and moans

28

through the room. It took a minute for me to regain myself, and while those seconds/minutes passed, everyone kind of talked to each other and cried. Finally, I just asked for one final confirmation.

"Everyone, wait. Please, just wait. OK, so what you're telling me is there is no brain activity, his eyes are fixed and dilated? There's…. He's not there? He's gone? What happens if you keep doing what you are doing? Is it going to make a difference? Is he going to wake up, or no?"

"We can work on him as long as you want us to; it is completely up to you, but no. There is not any activity, there's no stem activity. Ultimately, I think we will be asking you for a decision about continuing care every couple of hours. However, this is your decision alone, and we will do whatever it is you want us to do."

I stopped for a second. I took a deep breath…

"Stop. Just stop. If you're telling me that he's not going to wake up, if what you're doing isn't working, just stop. Quit."

I remember immediately looking to Andray, and getting a look of "I cannot believe you just said that" and instantaneously, an almost imperceptible nod. Then there was the immediate guilt of saying what I had to Dr. Melton. For a split second, I almost took the words back. I wanted in that instant to scream, "NO! NO! I'm wrong, go back in there and keep going, keep pushing!" In the second after that, my thought was "*No.* I can't do that to Jonce. He's *not* there; I can't try to prolong this just because *I* want him here. It's not fair, and I wouldn't want that if it was I, and I knew he wouldn't want that." So I remained silent, drowning in a sea of successive and relenting waves of guilt, fear of life without him, and, yes…. relief.

Admitting relief in this instance can seem really awful, uncaring, cold, and hateful… unless you have been exactly in this place. It's not relief of that person being gone; that's the last thing you want. It's the relief of not having to make more decisions and the relief that you have been able to make a decision to stop their pain. It's a floodgate of relief knowing you made the right decision, despite how wrong and oppressing it feels.

Quietly, everyone made one last trip to say goodbye, one last kiss, and one last "I love you." After everyone had had a turn and filed out,

I asked for a moment alone with my husband. Silent tears flowed down my face. I straightened out the blood soaked bandana still on his head and the blanket covering his body. I gently placed my forehead against his, and in a gentle whisper, I apologized. I apologized for everything he wouldn't be there to witness. I apologized to him for telling the doctors to stop. I apologized for everything that I wasn't as a wife and everything that we never got to be together.

Slowly, I leaned back, wiped my tears, and bent down for one small tender kiss on his lips, and an almost inaudible "I love you, thank you for marrying me." I turned, inhaled sharply, and faced his mother who had come in the room. I hugged her and waited in the hall. When I spotted the charge nurse, I went to him and thanked him for everything they had done to try to make this unbearable tragedy, bearable. Other nurses milled around, wiped tears from their own eyes, and went about tending to my husband. His mother clutched Jonce's work boots wrapped in a plastic bag. I clutched to her and we made our way back to the ICU waiting room.

During the last hours at the hospital, people milled around outside. They hugged one another, cried, and steadily made their way home. I waited a couple of extra hours to complete organ donation paperwork. This ended up being a fruitless effort, as Jonce's body was so racked with blunt force trauma that no part of his body was fit for donation; not even his eyes. During the time I spent waiting, I considered throwing myself off the building, I cried hysterically, I took small walks alone, hugged my friends, and called my Daddy with the news.

The last call I made was to our closest friends, known as the "The Boat Crew" (Cass, Jeff, Tina, Bart, Haley, Donny, Mark, Angela, Shonda, Wanda, and Ronnie W.). I am not sure which person in the group I called that night. I remember the call being short and to the point. I found out later, that all of them had gathered at the boat dock where we spent our weekends to await word on Jonce's condition. Other than the calls to my father, this was the hardest call I ever made during this whole time. Our friends had gathered to support one another, and I felt like my phone call to them unleashed a nuclear bomb.

By this time, only Becky was living with us, and she remained with me after everyone else had left. She asked if her sister (same mother, different father) could come get her and take her home. I told her this would be fine, and by 11:30 p.m., her sister had arrived at the entrance to the ER. After a heartfelt, yet awkward exchange, she promised to take Becky home to our house. I assured her I was right behind them, and I wouldn't be long. Becky was tired and she just wanted to sit in her daddy's recliner, and I needed the ride home alone to decompress.

I left about an hour after Becky and her sister. Windows rolled down, driving aimlessly through Birmingham; I called the house, and told Becky I was running a little behind. I was tired and drove slowly, and I took my time so I would get home safely. She sniffled a little and stated this was fine, and that she was just watching television. In a daze, I told her I loved her and hung up. I then called Jonce's cell phone several times just to hear his voice. I left him a voicemail, knowing he wouldn't receive it. I told him how much I loved him, and how I wanted him back with me. I don't remember the drive home.

When I got home, it was 3:30 a.m. in the morning. I saw Becky in the chair, and as I passed her, I grazed my fingers down her hair and told her I loved her. I then proceeded to mine and Jonce's bedroom. From the bench at the footboard, I gathered the last outfit Jonce had worn, a pair of khaki cargo shorts, a T-shirt, and a dirty pair of underwear. I clutched them to my chest, took the picture of us off the bedroom wall, and closed my door. I lay in the fetal position on his side of the bed, the radio crooning, as always, on the soft rock station, and sobbed. I kissed our picture, inhaled the scent of him as deeply as I could between sobs, and tried to sleep. Somewhere in time, my body gave out. I woke at 4:45 a.m. Upon waking, I stumbled from the bed and out my bedroom door still clutching his clothes. I saw Becky, and as I stumbled to the porch, I burst into tears, hyperventilated, and apologized to Becky for not being able to take care of her.

In retrospect, I think that may have frightened her, but she never let it show. I stumbled out to the front porch and spilled myself in one of two chairs where I would spend the next month of my life. Becky came out a few minutes later with a steaming cup of coffee in her hand. I don't remember if she said anything, but she hugged me and went back inside. I felt so guilty for sitting there. I needed to get up, take care of her, hug her, and make her breakfast, something… anything. However, the only thing I could do was look into the coffee cup as tears streamed down my face. The only thought I had was one that I heard once somewhere, a question that I asked someone at the hospital the night before. "How am I supposed to live in a world where he doesn't?"

2

A LITTLE ABOUT ME

1993-2010

Now that I have detailed the most tragic moment of my life, I think it is important for the reader to know about me. You know, a little background. This, at least to me, tends to make the author more emotionally accessible, even if only in my perception of who that author is. I think it will make the rest of the book more relevant to the reader and his or her own story. This is the *seriously* abbreviated version. I will focus heavily on certain things, but I promise not to bore you to death. I've been told on occasion that I tend to be outspoken. True. I have always spoken my mind, my heart, and usually anything else that tends to escape my lips. I write pretty much like I speak, so be prepared. God loves me just as I am, He works on me *constantly*, true enough, but He gave me a personality and a brain, so I tend to utilize them as often as possible. I am NOT perfect. In fact, I have been known to be a little "brash," but I am extremely lovable (humbly, I say). My best friend likes to remind me occasionally that I am brutally honest. It's a gift that I have. With this particular subject, blunt force honesty is probably best.

✧✧

You can go to the nearest bookstore and find "self-help books," books with "religious" overtones, "spiritual guidance," "handbooks," etc.... This is NOT one of those books. This is just me. This is my loss, my journey, and my personal experience with God. I have not always taken the right path, especially in my youth and early adulthood. At one point, I was so far from God, I could not have heard Him if He screamed in my ear. I am, as they say, "a work in progress" (Praise God and Thank you Jesus).

I spent the majority of my developmental years in Georgia with my parents and for periods, with my sister. To use the Southern phrase, "There's a whole mess of information there." We will not go into because it literally could consume chapters. Suffice it to say, my mom and stepdad (hereafter referred to as "daddy") were the most solid and loving parents a girl could ever want. God blessed me right off the bat with them. My natural father was absent many years of my life, and I never felt connected to him. We grew a little closer before his death, but my step daddy... IS DADDY. Most of you know what I mean. My sister was close to my natural father, and she lived with him for a few years, thus she was absent from my life for a time. However, my sister and I are closer now that we are both a little older. She is amazing I must say.

In a nutshell, I had a fabulous childhood. Very Norman Rockwell-ish. My parents and family are *the most* fabulous people. They are good hearted, sweet, nurturing, and God-fearing people. This reason alone is the reason why I think this journey has been as it has. I still have yet to find a word in the English language to adequately describe my journey. If I find one, I will let you know. I did well in school and enjoyed the geeky tasks most of my schoolmates did not care for. I had friends, good friends; a close-knit circle of undying camaraderie that extends to this day. I graduated high school with no fuss whatsoever and attempted college for about a semester and then quit. I wanted a "real job."

The "real jobs" were varied, mostly waitressing in one form or another, bartending, office manager positions, and a few other jobs that my father would disown me for writing about. Nothing seedy or illegal I might add, just not appropriate employment for his "baby girl." I am sure some of those jobs almost made him drop dead of a heart attack (this is that being far from God thing that I mentioned earlier). Also during this time, I dated several people, mom died, and I went back to college at age 23. I continue to attend college to this day, and I have acquired a collection of degrees that makes my Daddy proud, but also makes him shake his head. I can't help it; I'm a dork at heart, and I love to learn. Then I met Jonce.

As I stated earlier, my mother passed away in July of 2003. My ability to explain her loss in my life is not possible with human words, and in some ways, it is the reason I push myself as I do. When I miss her, I dive in with the tenacious quality of a piranha at feeding time, and those that enter the path of destruction can often find themselves missing an appendage. Shortly before her diagnosis, my dad had gotten back into motorcycling and brought mom and me into the fold of a family we know as the Southern Cruisers Riding Club (SCRC).

A band of average Americans who love and adore the open road and the freedom that comes only on two wheels. The SCRC would become our extended family and they would see my family through the worst time in our lives. Dad even attempted, at some point, to school my mother on the finer points of motorcycling by trying to teach her to ride her own motorcycle. In practicing in the mechanics of operation, she gunned the throttle, popped the clutch, and pitched it to the left. I was not there for the actual event, but my mother told me later, she *heard* her leg break before she even hit the ground. That was the beginning and the end of her experience as a cyclist. However, she did remain daddy's faithful passenger until too sick to continue.

Shortly after her death, I took up the hobby myself. I did this for several reasons. The love of motorcycling, the friendships made with the other riders, a need to feel closer to my dad in the wake of my mother's death, and the sheer excitement of riding with my father on a mountain road. He could handle the bike flawlessly, but it still freaked me out. I have learned through my own limited experience with motorcycles that there is a certain degree of trust when it comes to riding. I trust my dad implicitly; it's the terrain that scares me. I would rather have control, a noticeably repeated theme in my life.

Oil and perfume rejoice the heart; so does the sweetness of a friend's counsel that comes from the heart.

Proverbs 27: 9(NIV)

Influential Friends & Family

Before donning waders and trolling on any further into the depths of this book, I should first give some kudos to those in my *earthly* life that are, at least in part, the reason I am writing. Those closest to me, those who truly know who I am as a person, and have influenced me in ways I never expected. I have several of those people in my life, and they deserve a mere mention. These people are my tethers that keep me centered in for reality. They are the people who are my lifelines more often than I care to admit. I realize that even if I occasionally become resentful, wanting to cut the lifelines, or getting clothes lined by them, if these people were not in my life, I'd already be dead in the water.

Mom

In retrospect, my mother (rest her soul) was one of the few people in my life who defended me in my decision not to have children. Despite her innate connection with God and her quest to be a good Christian woman, she staunchly defended me against the onslaught from others about my literal and biblical lots in life. Granted, she would have fainted away in my "Marriage and the Family" class as an undergraduate.

In this class, I intentionally sparked a debate with a nice Mormon woman (and the three other pregnant women who were also matriculating) in my class on the assumption that women were put solely on earth to procreate ceaselessly. Suffice it to say the "healthy debate" in class did not cause spontaneous labor, and no pregnant women were harmed in completing the semester long class with me. My mother never did hear of the rumblings of the debate. However, in the end, I think she might have been proud of me. While my philosophical viewpoints would have differed from hers, and she would have used the bible to respectfully disagree, she would have stood by my right to defend my position.

Daddy

Daddy. I love my daddy more than any one person on earth, and will, until one of us passes this earthly plane. He is the epitome of a great parent, as was my mother, and my step mom, Pam. Daddy took my sister and me on at the tender age of twenty-five. Bless him. He had *NO* idea what he was getting into. That having been said, he parented us flawlessly, and I can say this in all honesty, despite any minor missteps *he* feels *he* may have taken in the early years of parenthood. The man is patient and kind. He is relentless in his ability to guide, forgive, and let a child make her own mistakes. He is truly a man of God, and I was blessed for him to have been brought into my life.

I thought when I married Jonce I would be able to replicate his parental example. I have had a much harder time with that than I ever thought I would. As the saying goes, I am "not cut from that cloth." Daddy is made from silk, I fall more into the burlap category. I have little patience, I am testy when I shouldn't be, but I am forgiving and tend to overlook or excuse things. This man, this father that didn't have to be, has my undying love and respect.

Heather

Heather, my non-biological, "stands between you and oncoming traffic, bff/sister" for almost twenty-three years is also a saving grace in my life. She knows my "maternal instinct" was not very strong. Heather has three of her own and I love them all dearly, I just couldn't handle them (or any child really) more than two hours before it felt like my nerves have been run through a meat grinder. She knows this, and tolerates my flaws. She is a saint, and she continually astounds my sensibilities and definitions of true friendship. In her words, "Oh, honey, you're not a bad woman, you just aren't hard-wired like that. Motherhood's just not your--- *your thing.*"

Oddly, Heather is a friend that I wouldn't have guessed I would ever have had. In high school we were really more "acquaintances" than friends until the end of our junior year. Essentially, we didn't think "highly" of one another, but we had mutual friends, so in the end, bygones. Later in life, beyond high school, we became lifelong friends. She is akin to my personal counselor, which I find to be incredibly insightful. I love Heather. Her ability to "call me on it" is heartwarming if not ever so slightly annoying.

Besides being annoyingly insightful, she is also that person in my life who is endlessly forgiving and nurturing. Living in a small two-bedroom apartment together was one of the best experiences of my life to date. She fed me, cared for me when I was sick and even argued with my mother. The day she argued with my mother, I realized how brave Heather was. While other friends are also a constant in my life, like Jody, Heather and I have a "sister" friendship; its bond is life long and tougher than anything else in my life is.

Heather is the one who will sit in the freezing cold on the back porch with you while you vent incessantly, smoke cigarettes, and complain. She has the uncanny ability to nod, narrow her eyes, and can tell you without actually saying the words "you're being a moron, cut the bull, and get real." For all of us, any of us, a friend such as this is a rarity, and they are precious and profound. For the record, Heather and I are a package deal. Women know precisely what I mean by this. When a man marries a woman, they automatically get the BFF; it's a rule. Jonce used to say Heather was my other half sometimes and the only one who could rein me in when I acted like a complete idiot. I miss that man. Jonce loved her too, and that just made him *more* endearing.

Jody

Jody is amazing, beautiful, and a true tether who keeps me grounded. She is also responsible for my nickname, Gette (pronounced "Jet"); a derivative of my first name, Bridgette. She is incredibly cerebral, can analyze a topic to death, and she is frightfully insightful about men. We get along well on this account due to both of us being extremely analytical. I speak with her more on the marital aspects of my life; Heather handles more of the parental aspects. Jody is the friend you want when marriage has ceased to be blissful. She will come in with square-toed boots and defend you until the walls of Jericho are breached.

Staunchly defensive, she is a friend every woman should have. The one who will listen to you moan and complain. She will clearly defend you in all of your marital relationship faux pas, and then lay out the other side of the argument in such a way that you know you *just were told you did everything very wrong, still defends you for doing it, and then scoots you on your way, knowing you have to apologize.*

Jody is the friend who proclaimed she would never marry and never have children. It was mostly my wedding that tipped the scales in the opposite direction for her though. She got the "marriage bug" there, and I take full responsibility. She was married, had a baby, and then divorced a short time later. In retrospect, she doesn't regret having being married, and wouldn't give her baby up for the world. However, she is also keenly aware and respectful, that while I don't mind being a stepparent, I don't want to actually have a child. She doesn't use the "Oh, it would be different if you had one" mantra.

Shane

Shane was the brother-in-law extraordinaire. He came to live with us after he got divorced from his wife. I was incredibly leery at first, as I was already worn out from having most of my stepchildren in the house. It originally appeared to be that I would have a middle-aged, unemployed child camping out in my living room. I could not have been more wrong.

The initial week or so took some getting used to, but in the end, Shane proved to be a staunch supporter of mine, read my signals of stress better than most, and has no children of his own. He understands the perspective I come from. He was quick to point out when I needed to ease up, step back, or force others to handle their own issues. Shane always told me "You do too much for everyone." Shane was also very aware that Jonce and I needed "us time" and was always willing to give us that opportunity to perform marriage maintenance by watching the kids and the house so we could get away.

In addition, Shane turned out to be an incredible chef. He also did laundry, cleaned floors, and cleaned the bathroom. He was only unemployed for about the first six months of his stay, and then was employed as a full time chef at a local bar/eatery. Even after gainful employment, I don't remember cooking or cleaning much. When he became unemployed a second time, I was again banished from my own kitchen and the toils of grocery shopping. In addition, he also listened to me complain in a relentless fashion. I swear his patience was astounding. He told me not long ago that he considers me the closest thing to a blood sister he will ever have. Maybe having a 175-pound live in unemployed (again) child in the home did have its perks.

Tammie, Jimmy, Angela, Ali, Kelsey, and Christie.

Jonce had many relatives, many of which were related to him by marriage. Jimmy was Jonce's cousin, but he was also one of Jonce's closest and dearest friends. We spent many weekends with Jimmy and his wife Angela. We would watch football games, NASCAR races, or just spend time together enjoying each other's company. Tammie is Jimmy's sister, and probably one of the sweetest, most fun individuals I have EVER had the pleasure of knowing. Her heart is big and her support of me after Jonce died was nothing short of amazing. Ali, Kelsey, and Christie, I consider almost one unit at times. These three women were a support to me in ways I can't even begin to describe. They supported me not only after Jonce's death, but in the times when I had issues in my marriage, work, or school that literally made my head spin. These three women have been and continue to be a blessing in my life. Ali was a confidant to me in times when all I wanted to do was give up. She endlessly loved me and provided me the proverbial shoulder more times than I care to admit. She always did so in love and always helped me to get my feet back under me. The thing that strikes me most about this group of friends and family is that there isn't anything you can't tell them. Often times you don't have to *tell* them anything. They just know. After someone you love dies, that can be the most valuable and underestimated comfort.

Jason and B.J.

Jason and B.J. are Jonce's brother and sister-in-law. I don't list them separately because I have never seen them as separate. One is part of the other. If you stripped one away from the other, the picture isn't complete; you only get half of the story. B.J. and Jason are as outspoken as they come. They will tell you without hesitation what they think, they speak bluntly, and both are fiercely protective of the ones they love. They have more personality in their little fingers than most people express over the course of a lifetime.

B.J. is also funny, beautiful, loving, and she is a fantastic mother. B.J. has the gentlest heart. I love her more than anything, and often refer to her as "My B.J." The day I lost Jonce, she was the only person I wanted. When I had "parental issues," I preferred opinions from B.J. because she not only knows me, but she knows the family. If she had not been there for me when times were hard, I don't know what I would have done.

Jason is my brother. Blood or not, he will *always* be my brother. There isn't a descriptive term I have for Jason that would completely give you a sense of who he is. When you get around him, his personality is magnetic and his laugh is contagious. Now more than I ever have before, I love to hear him laugh. It reminds me of Jonce, but it has a different quality to it altogether. His laugh gives comfort and joy when you hear it. It's like being wrapped in a warm blanket while you hold your favorite teddy bear.

Having B.J. and Jason in my life has been a huge blessing to me even if they don't realize it. They are stellar examples of how you should be married, how to communicate, and how well two people can know and love one another. Both of them are simply amazing. I know that even though Jonce is gone and life moves forward, if I ever needed either of them for anything, they would be there. No questions asked.

3

$\mathcal{J}$ONCE

2003-2010

"Let him kiss me with the kisses of his mouth-For your love is better than wine."
Song of Solomon 1:2 (NIV)

Riding became part of my identity in 2003, and I can honestly say it is one of the most relaxing and enjoyable experiences. I refer to it as 650 ccs of therapy, but currently I don't ride. I rode with Jonce, and after he passed, it felt *wrong* to ride without him. However, Jonce told me, the fact that I rode of my own volition, on my *own* bike, was one of the main reasons my husband fell in love with me. After my mom passed in 2003, I went to the "Dothan Peanut Festival" in Alabama with my father. Dothan is where approximately four or five bikers of the SCRC took credit for introducing me to my husband. Really, it was astounding he even talked to me, because my first words could have been construed as an insult.

I walked up to the bar and was introduced to several people, my husband included. I thought I felt my heart skip. He looked like a total bad boy, and I thought that my dad must have lost his mind bringing me to this place. I looked him up and down when we were introduced, "Tigger (that's me), this is Devil Dog" (Jonce). Who introduced us specifically, I cannot remember exactly. As I mentioned, several people to this day take credit, but I distinctly remember looking him over and thinking, "Hhhmmm... Devil Dog huh? I wonder if he actually bites?" I found out later that night that his handle, "Devil Dog," was a reference to the four plus years he served in the military as a U.S. Marine. My attraction to him (even before I knew what Devil Dog meant) increased exponentially. The look, the posture, the little knowing smile, ooh yeah, this one was going to get me good. I had no idea.

He had a "do-rag" on his head, cute jeans, his riding vest (complete with vest patches from places I had yet to ride), a tight shirt, and a look of... I am not sure how to word it. I almost sensed a dare emanating from him to make a smart remark; a regular hello wasn't going to get this man's attention. Being the sucker I am, I took the bait.

I said, "Hhhhmmm, you don't even look old enough to ride."

I then casually moved down the bar as I was being introduced to other SCRC members. My dad looked mortified (although he smiled a little), and the other bikers looked flabbergasted and thoroughly entertained at my initial quip. Jonce looked floored, pointed to his vest and said,

"HEY! It says 'Road Captain!'"

I looked one more time, and stated,

"So it does."

I continued to mingle with my newfound friends for the better part of two hours. I actually considered these bikers as family members, after all they did for our family, during my mother's illness. After about two hours, Jonce approached me at the table and asked if my dad had gone to the room to go to bed. I told him, "Yeah, its' safe, you can sit down." My ability to be coy and adorable is not very strong, but if I turn it on, I can turn it on. When I want to flirt, I know how to do so, and I am able to do it well. In my opinion, all women have an innate flirting gene. It manifests itself with the hair and head toss, the slight grazing of fingers along the neck and hair, the half look from under the eyelashes. Really, it doesn't take much effort, especially if you have the advantage of everyone who knows him providing you encouragement. I am still unclear if using your womanly wiles to attract a mate is a sin of the flesh or not, but again, in those days, I was still far from where I needed to be.

Later, we decided to troll the hotel parking lot looking and look at everyone's motorcycles. He seemed impressed I rode my own when I pointed it out. We turned down the sidewalk, continued on (he planned the whole thing I am sure of it now, though he adamantly denied it), and came to stop in front of a particularly impressive machine. The colors in the tribal paint job were extraordinary and the bike heavy laden with chrome accessories. I enviously gazed bike and made the comment on how impressive I thought it was. Let's face it; my motorcycle was akin to a coffee pot on two wheels. This was a motorcycle of epic proportions. Jonce looked at me and said, "It's mine."

I eyed him suspiciously, as the moment of realization hit me. He guided me this entire way to get to this point! Thus, I quickly started a mental calculation of the odds that his room was within spitting distance. Generally, bikers keep their machine (even among friends) within eyeshot of their hotel window. The machines are like children to those of us that ride. Messing with another (wo)man's bike is analogous to eating the birthday kid's last piece of cake. You just don't do it.

As we walked, I made a suggestion to walk back to the bar in order for me to visit the ladies room…***BAM!***

He said, "My room is two more doors down this way, you can use mine if you'd like."

He could have denied that evening's happenings until pigs fly and the cows came home, but I know the truth. I may be a few pennies shy in change for common sense, but I'm no dummy either.

I wandered back into my hotel room at four in the morning just as the birds started to rustle. This seemed somewhat disconcerting for my father. Face down on his queen size bed closest to the door, fully dressed in riding gear, boots, hat, and vest; a small mumble came from the bed. Apparently, he had been walking around earlier in the evening when I hadn't come back to the room.

"Where have you been?"

"Ummm, outside walking the parking lot, looking at bikes with Devil Dog."

"Yeah, try again; I have circled the parking lot four or five times, *two* hours ago."

Mortified would be an accurate description of how I felt. However, the giddiness of having met someone that made me feel like Jonce did acted as a daddy-proof buffer.

"We just hung out, OK, oh, and he kissed me, OK? Gheesh, Dad."

For the record, I promise that's all that happened, a little kissing, some hand holding, and TV watching. I behaved, as a proper lady biker should, thank you very much.

This was quickly followed by a quick peck to my dad's cheek, and a mad dash in the bathroom to dress in jammies and hit the other queen bed. As I entered the bathroom, I detected a small moan that only a father can make upon receiving such news. Poor Daddy. He told me after Jonce and I had been dating a while that he couldn't take me anywhere, because apparently, "I liked to bring things home with me."

"My lover spoke and said, "Arise, my darling, my beautiful one, and come with me"
Song of Solomon 2:10(NIV)

Courtship

From this point forward, Jonce and I dated back and forth between Alabama and Georgia for nine months. On our first date, he made me privy to the fact that he had four children by three different women, and had been married three times (two times to the same woman). Yeah, I know, it seemed convoluted and a little breathtaking to me too. Don't get me wrong, I hardly think the man was reckless or ill equipped to handle parenting. However, I do think that he was young and carefree and was not particularly well guided in the use of contraception early in life. I have no question that his intentions and advice to me were based in love and a sense of experience. However, I took issue with being told how I should feel or how I should handle issues with the children by someone who had difficulty and made mistakes with step parenting themselves; those who live in glass houses should not throw stones (or in this case boulders). Put more plainly, I don't think it's wise for a person to use the phrase "when I was a step-parent, I ..." (this would be said boulder).

I believe that repeated and unsolicited advice such as this can alienate someone in the parenting capacity. When my parenting style or decision-making became an "issue" for him (both pre-marital and afterwards), I can honestly say, I am not sure I cared a great deal. Not that he didn't have valuable advice, but the sub-text was condescending. If I strike you as a person who responds well to condescension, you need to reread this book from the beginning.

My experiences step-parenting were different from Jonce's, the children were different, and I was different. Let a person vent for goodness sake. He was a wonderful husband and a capable parent, but giving advice to a person who has never step-parented or had children of their own should be handled with a certain amount of finesse, especially during the courtship phase. God, I love(d) my husband, but finesse was not so much his forte.

Again though, someone else's experience was not necessarily my experience. His experience came from having participated in creating children, step parenting other people's children, and having been a stepchild himself. Prior to marrying him, I had only two of these experiences under my belt. I think he understood my point of view more clearly after we married and there were three children living in the home. Partially, I believe this was due to an increase in our honest communication and participation in couples counseling.

Also during our courtship, I was an undergraduate in my last year at Georgia State University, and was scheduled to graduate in August 2004. After I graduated, I was accepted to five graduate programs, none of which was in Alabama. I used to think this was Murphy's Law in action; I have since realized this had to have been God's providence. Jonce had stated he would go with me to Virginia, as the graduate program at Marymount University was my first choice. I toyed with this idea, and he did appear rather serious in committing to move. We later put a stop to the notion because of the children. Although he was not a full-time parent, he still needed to be local and be able to be with his children, so I moved. I mean, I picked up everything I knew, had, and cherished, and moved to podunkville, Alabama.

Now look, I love Alabama, specifically Lake Guntersville. It is open, rural, quiet, slower paced than Atlanta, and frankly, littered with cows. I have a fascination with cows that I have yet to mention, but I do have one. I think they are incredibly adorable and look so stupid they are cute. No, I am not a vegan, vegetarian, or whatever the politically correct term is these days. While I love and adore cows, and think they are the cutest thing (and I mean the cutest thing *ever*), I also like them wrapped in cellophane at the local market. Hey, it's the grand circle of life sweetheart; you can't be emotionally connected to your food, your pets yes, your steak, no.

That having been said, the move to Alabama was a traumatic culture shock, to say the least. I moved over here, bought a house,

Jonce moved in, and I did not have a graduate program to call my own. I looked diligently for a year and decided on a program at the University of Alabama in Huntsville. A Masters of Arts in Experimental Research appeared to be my destiny. Originally, I considered a clinical degree, but once I told myself there was no way I would be able to conquer the intricacies of research, I sealed my fate. If I tell myself it can't be done, it's as good as decided that's what I will end up doing. It all goes back to that control thing I referred to earlier.

In the end, I obtained my Masters Degree from UAH, and have since completed a doctoral program at Walden University. Praise God! I tend to bore easily, and used to use school as an escape mechanism from the roles in my life with which I am uncomfortable. My therapist Jan used to be amazed at my ability to be insightful about my own life. She thought it funny that I had the knowledge I needed, but was too hesitant or too freaked out to do anything about such. Now, if I become freaked out or I drag my feet on doing what I know I should do, I utilize my church family and bible study group for support and encouragement. Jan is still a wonderful and dear friend. Her support and encouragement have been immeasurable to me.

My therapist and I didn't gloss over anything. Now I deal with things that bother me, and I don't use school as an escape route. It is amazing how much more clearly schoolwork and writing have become since I made that change. But I digress. While in the graduate program, from the fall of 2005 through the summer of 2007, I also worked full time. I started out with a temp agency doing payroll fifty-five miles from our home, and then opted to take a lesser paying job closer to the house that was at least somewhat related to my degree in psychology. I changed jobs one more time after this, and remained a faithful employee of the state of Alabama from 2006 to 2012.

In order to get the full gist of my life, let me detail some specific events that shaped me up until the time we married.

Memphis

Jonce and I met, we courted, I moved my life to Alabama, we moved in together (again, I was far from God). I started my Masters program, and we rode motorcycles. Life was humming along. After I had moved to Alabama and established employment, we went to a huge national SCRC convention in Memphis. During the onslaught of the remnants of Hurricane Ivan in 2005, we bravely (or some may say, insanely) climbed aboard his motorcycle together, and headed out to meet 500 of our closest friends. Somehow, we made it there alive.

I wasn't taking my own bike because I was a) too inexperienced, b) NOT driving my bike during a hurricane, and c) absolutely not taking responsibility for my own death due to transportation choices. I told him that if we were going to die on the trip there, he was going to be the fall guy. Period. He assured me no such thing would happen, and for me to load up. Bless him.

Having driven through what had to have been 45 mph winds, with 65 mph gusts, we made it to Iuka, Mississippi when the chain snapped off the bike. Now, due to my husband's accessory fetish/mental illness for his monster of a bike, our lives were saved. Had he not had these atrocious wheel covers, it is a sure bet the chain would have slung off, snaked in the tire spokes, and hurled us to certain death. However, the worst that happened was a large jerking motion forward, and a coasting stop in front of (I am not kidding) a *small church* on a hill with a side awning (I am quite certain I mentioned God's providence earlier – Well there you go). We managed to get the bike up a steep hill and under the awning, and we located a small motorcycle store five minutes before it closed.

The owner sent some poor chump out in the driving rain with a toolbox, and a new chain. Seriously? This would have never happened in any other circumstances. First, the chain was a third of what it would have cost nearer to our home. Second, they sent some poor boy to put the chain on, and third, all of this was completed in a hurricane. That amazes me to this day.

In all our soaking glory, we remounted, and finally made it to Memphis, totally unscathed. The National Rally was a blast. Bikers were running amuck, partying under the viaduct of the interstate, karaoke singing, dancing. All good harmless fun. You wouldn't think the words "biker" and "harmless" can be synonymous, but with this particular group, yes, it can.

The next morning, we wandered to get breakfast and see fellow bikers. This was a period in my life when I chose to drink - rather excessively on occasion. Not a choice I am proud of, but it is what it is, and I don't begrudge anyone who does drink, it's just not what I choose anymore. All morning, all I heard was, "Tigger, you look rough baby, go take a nap." I must have heard it twenty times in the course of an hour and a half. WHY did everyone want me to take a nap? I mean, I didn't look my best, but Gheesh, I didn't look like the living dead either. Well, that was to become apparent at the convention dinner later that night.

After I caved and took the nap that everyone had nagged me about all morning, I woke, and Jonce and I dressed in our finest leathers and jeans and headed to the convention center. We proceeded to partake of overpriced rubber chicken with limp vegetables, and dessert that can give you a cavity from twenty paces. Through dinner, the silent auction, and awards, we mingled, laughed, drank, and had a wonderful time.

Finally, at the end of the night, dressed in stupid, large furry hats from our earlier trip to Beale Street, the Alabama group was called on stage. I was dragged up, as I was considered a transplant from the Georgia group. On stage, it soon became apparent, there was an altogether different reason our group was singled out. Literally, only fifteen seconds before I realized what was happening, I sought my father's face out of the audience and locked in on my Daddy. He was grinning bigger than I had ever seen him grin, and then Jonce dropped to one knee to ask me to be his bride.

The rest is mostly a blur, other than my stammered answer of "YES!" Mind you, the best part of this was the sneakiest, slimy, and romantic way this had been pieced together. Jonce had apparently secretly met with my father to get my late mother's wedding ring. I found out later my dad almost wrecked twice getting to Memphis, and also stopped and had to move a tree from the road. He was also several hours late in arriving due to the inclement weather. However, watching your daughter be proposed to in front of 500 whooping and hollering bikers is apparently worth almost being killed. *Now* do you see why I love my daddy so much?

Engagement

OK, so now engaged, we return to normal life - for a minute. Several months later, as we planned a no-fuss wedding in the Tennessee Smoky Mountains, I find out that Jonce's third wife wasn't having any of this. She really didn't know he had gotten engaged, but when your fiancé calls and tells you his last divorce isn't legal, a girl just assumes that the previous wife has actually been aware, and intentionally tried to wreak havoc on our lives. Was that an unfair assumption? In retrospect, yes, I can say that it is, but at the time, that's how it felt. *Apparently*, when you get divorced, you have to sign your *married* name, not your *maiden* name on the papers. So naturally, the wedding was postponed, and we had to track her down to get the papers properly signed.

Children

I honestly believe, I was not meant to have children. We can argue all day about one's biblical obligation to procreate, but it's just how I feel. I did not want kids, and well… he had four. Jonce indicated we would have the kids every other weekend, which was great. I could most assuredly handle that, no problem. This is not about all of the children, just about one's arrival onto the scene. I had met Daniel, Jonce's third child and youngest son, during our dating season. Now, I loved Jonce immensely, but he had not always been the most present parent (and the first to admit such). He had a bout in which he made poor choices and found himself unable to contend with being a parent. Thus, Daniel lived with his grandparents. Becky, Jonce's youngest child and only girl, lived with her mother and grandmother. Brad, Jonce's second oldest child, lived with his mother and stepfather. Michael, Jonce's oldest child, also lived with his mother and stepfather. Michael and Daniel shared the same mother, but Brad and Becky's mothers were different women. I realize this all seems a bit confusing, but suffice it to say, at the time we met and courted, Jonce and I did not have a child living with us full time.

We must have been living together just four to six months when the nuke was dropped. Now, I was clear when we dated that I didn't want to *have* kids, although I was totally fine with having Jonce's kids part time (at least to begin with). I was very quick to point out that I was capable of some parenting, and a part time arrangement seemed feasible. Jonce never indicated from the beginning that the children were going to move in. At least not before we got married. Don't get me wrong, it's not that I didn't like the kids. I did (and do), but I hadn't known them, and they hadn't known me long enough feel that I was the most obvious choice for Stepmother of the Year just yet. We weren't even engaged at this point.

We had spent some time together, sure, but not massive quantities. Well, I never got the chance to ease into anything. At this point, we were living together and life was blissfully moving along. One night we sat on the porch, listening to the crickets and the nighttime sounds of the neighborhood, just chatting about work and life. Then he told me. Now, I don't remember the exact words, because as soon as they were uttered the only sound was my blood rushing through my own veins, and the once comforting sound of crickets now sounded like screeching sirens.

In short, Daniel was moving in. Nine-year-old Daniel. I am at this point, nearing thirty, and the most practical experience I have had with a kid this age, was well, *me* at age nine. *I didn't even like me at nine.*

Oh, it gets better, wait for it…. He's moving in. ***Tomorrow.***

I know an argument ensued, because I remember walking into the house and him flying after me, almost removing the storm door from the hinges. I couldn't even begin to tell what was said during the argument. All I know was that I felt like I was sinking, and he wasn't pulling me out, he was throwing a seventy-five pounds, sweet adorable little redheaded anvil on my head, and nagging at me to quit complaining.

I soon calmed, and we eventually agreed that given the circumstances (and still, I am not even sure to this day, what those were), Daniel would move in. I caved. I was afraid to upset the man I loved, that he would take this as some rejection of him or his children, I gunny-sacked my discontent, my anger, my fear, sucked it up and moved on. In retrospect, I know that this was incredibly unfair to him, and I should not have just "let it go." We should have delayed the move for a while and really discussed how things were going to work. Jonce would admit it himself that springing the move-in on me was unfair, and he apologized for it later.

In retrospect, I think Daniel's move in to our home was intense, and I felt completely overwhelmed. This, incidentally, brought about fears I had always had about being a parent; I feared being responsible for another *human being*, I feared I was going to mess his kid up, I feared rejection from Jonce, the kids, and his family. I feared that if I said I wasn't ready, or I said "no," it would have cost me my relationship. I was never more closed off than I was that night, and I am woman enough to admit it. I have a bad history of accommodating others. Accommodating is also another form of burying the things that make me angry. I used to push my fears and anger down, forget about what was making me angry or fearful, or just overlook the things that brought out these feelings. I buried these things so I wouldn't have to contend with them, no matter the justification I might actually have. I didn't see it then, and sometimes, I still don't see it in me now. I have to take "inventory" of myself. Geesh. My therapist and her self-realization techniques.

Educational Attainment

I started my Masters Program before we married, and concluded the degree afterwards, but it begs attention. My husband was a saint on earth, in my eyes. I read somewhere that many marriages dissolve because of a graduate program. I totally believe this. Maintaining ones sanity in a graduate level program, at a research university no less, is stress like no other. Jonce endured endless nights of my writing papers, my making smart-alecky remarks for no reason other than fatigue, and my crying fits because of misplaced commas in my thesis. In addition, my attitude during my seventh draft of my thesis was enough to make even Jonce burst into tears. Remember the movie Fatal Attraction? Do you remember when Glen Close totally loses it? Compared to me, she was an amateur who couldn't act herself out of a wet paper sack. Jonce's support and encouragement during those times qualified him for Sainthood I tell you. The kudos in the dedication was not even a scratch on the surface of my gratitude.

4

$\mathcal{M}$ARITAL BLISS... LOL

Marriage is a wonderful gift from God. Period. Jonce was, and will always be to me, a gracious, sweet, wonderful, loving, and caring husband. Now, don't get me wrong, marriage wasn't always unicorns and rainbows. On more than one occasion, I assure you, it felt like Armageddon had arrived, and I had missed the news bulletin it was coming. Marriages have problems, ups, downs, fights, make-ups, and everything in between. You don't just get married, stay googly-eyed, and set up shop at Cinderella's castle. Eventually, reality, children, and the daily grind sets in. Maintaining a marriage in the midst of all this is challenging.

Hopefully, after the fairy tale myth blows up in ones face like a nuclear bomb, there is someone whom you actually _like;_ someone whom you _know_ is going to be there for the long haul. Hopefully, you have that one man who still loves you (let alone still wants to be in the same room with you) when your morning is a disaster of BAD hair, unshaven legs, no coffee, complaints, and demanding children... well... the man's a keeper.

I won't bore you with the all details of the wedding, just the outline version. We wanted simple. I mean I wanted to ENJOY my day, not plan myself into the ICU with a bleeding ulcer. We decided a wedding in Gatlinburg was the ticket. We invited bikers and regular folks alike to the wedding. Guests were told they could dress very casual or as dolled up as they wanted to be, so long as they did not look prettier than I did (bikers showed in leathers and do-rags).

Everything was arranged, and all I had to do was get my hair, make up done, and show up to slide into my dress. Ta-DA!!! No muss, no fuss. The crowd wasn't big, but the important people were there. Most importantly, Jonce did not pass out, or throw up during the ceremony. Jonce told me later that his knees kept shaking and his nerves were frayed, and that he asked the staff at the chapel if he could have a stool to sit on during the ceremony. When they came and actually asked me if this was permissible, I unleashed both my father and sister. Jonce was confused about why he was so nervous. He didn't seem to understand why. My sister told him, "The reason you're nervous, is because you got it right this time." Bless her heart. I love that woman.

The wedding was simple, sweet, and good fun. I didn't pass out from excitement, Jonce didn't have to sit during the vows, and no small children threw up, knocked over candles, or cried incessantly during the nuptials. Countless pictures were taken and the day was crystal clear and a balmy sixty-five degrees. It was perfect. We all then went to a local restaurant and had a "Dutch" reception. If you could make it and buy your own food, then come on! I am so glad that we chose the venue we did to get married. We didn't have to pay thousands of dollars for the headaches of planners, obnoxious cakes, horrible bridesmaid dresses, and a reception dinner with rubber chicken and dry vegetables. I think a lot can be said for the sage old advice from several people before getting married – "Do yourselves a favor; keep it simple, the important part is the *MARRIAGE, NOT THE WEDDING.*"

Everyday Life

Honeymoon concluded, we returned home and back to reality. Oh Joy. Work, friends, families, get-togethers, parties, children, bills, budgets, stress, friends, beer drinking, races, football games, the construction of a new home, and the list goes on. As an aside, I highly recommend one does NOT build a new home in the first year of marriage. The first year is hard enough without having to deal with a slightly obsessive-compulsive husband in regards to construction and contractors. However, this was my life, this is the way it went, and I wouldn't have had it any other way.

We had fun, we laughed, we cried, became sad, angry, and happy again. The world keeps on spinning and the bills keep on coming. And so did the children. We originally started with Daniel in 2005, and then Becky was added to the household after Jonce gained custody of her in 2007. By 2008, Michael moved in for his senior year of high school, so now we are up to three. During 2008, when Michael moved in, Daniel moved back to his grandparent's house (Jonce's father and stepmother). So now, we were back to two children.

Uncle Shane still resided in the home, but he was gone more often than not due to work and spending quality time with his sweetie. Jonce traveled quite a bit with work, and I worked a minimum of forty hours per week at the local Department of Human Resources. I would get up, take Becky to school, work, pick her up at her grandfather's (the same household where her brother Daniel was residing), go home, clean house, cook dinner, and work on my homework. When Jonce got home, there would be time for me to take a small break. After this small reprieve, I would then get back to work on homework. Then I would have time for some kissy face with Jonce, a shower, and then bed. Rinse and repeat from 2006 - July 2010.

My Work

When I moved to Alabama, I worked as a temp in payroll fifty-five miles from the house, then changed jobs a few months later for lesser pay but I was closer to home. I stayed with the mental health center for about a year, and then ended up doing social work for the county's child abuse and neglect division. Work hummed along fine for me, but by 2008, the stress increased because I had been moved from the grant-based family preservation division to the child abuse and neglect division.

I took my work home with me, I cried, became angry with people, and on some days, I was just unbearable to live with. Period. Jonce was attentive to my moods with work, and tried to help me relax as best as he could. Other days, he would listen to me rant and rave, but he never tried to give me advice; he just let me vent until I felt better. However, by 2009 he was more adamant about me making a career move that would be less stressful.

He understood that I had to finish school (by this time I was a Ph.D. candidate) in order to do this, but I think seeing me stressed out hurt his heart, and it did take a toll on my ability to be sympathetic and caring sometimes. Other times, I cared entirely too much. I would take home work, take phone calls with clients, midnight runs on call, or just because someone needed me. Work leaks in if you don't closely monitor yourself; it will suck you in, and suck you dry. In the end, your family suffers for it.

I finally relented and actively started searching for other work, but not in Alabama. This set off a tiff or two, but in the end, he agreed that if he could find work out of state as well, it was definitely an option. Ultimately, nothing came of the job search and we remained in Alabama, and I remained with the Department of Human Resources. I continued in this field until just recently. Now away from this job, I have much less stress, and I feel like I am in a place that God not only provided, but also practically insisted on my being.

Why the change happened *after* his death, I don't know. I don't question it, and I don't fight God's will. He takes care of me and I relent to Him to do His will, not mine. He knows better than I do. I am but a thread in His tapestry, I've decided that I will know His reasons on a need-to-know basis, and apparently, right now, I don't need to know.

Jonce's Work

When I met Jonce, he was working as a parts manager for a motorcycle shop. He continued working there until 2006, when he went back into the telecommunications business.

When I say, "telecommunications business," I do not mean the IT Department or working at the telephone company. Jonce climbed towers, maintained structures reaching hundreds or thousands of feet in the air. He was a "Tower Dog," AKA, Tower Climber. Crazy Person. Adrenaline Junkie. Thrill Seeker. Mad Man. He loved his job, and I mean *loved* it. Like with any other job, there were frustrations, and he would get livid because of old or worn out equipment, poor attitudes, or boneheaded decisions on a worksite, but overall he loved that job like no other. I think it fed the former Marine mentality in him. He identified so strongly with his service in the USMC that, in some ways, I think the Tower Dog job gave him a similar adrenaline rush and a sense of camaraderie that being in the Marines did. A tower crew isn't just a team who work together, they are a tightly wound bunch of brothers and/or sisters. Jonce got into that line of work, thanks to a friend with which he served. Jonce said it was a wonderful job, and he found being three hundred to over a thousand feet off the ground peaceful. I found the mere idea terrifying. You say tomato; I say to-mah-toe.

He was a safe and studious project manager and he loved and respected his tower crew like brothers. The feeling was mutual. I told him more than once that if he did want to quit (these were the days of high frustration) to go ahead and quit, go back to school, go back to the motorcycle industry, or whatever he wanted. We would manage to find a way. Normally his frustration would pass quickly, and he would be ready to attack the towers again with new vigor. The one thing he did hate about the job was the travel. He told me once that when you are single and you travel that much, it's no big deal, but he hated leaving for two to four weeks at a time, and I hated for him to walk out the door.

He also told me that he would come off the towers as soon as I was able to land another job, or if he could find an alternative, which paid what he was making at the time. The new house had over extended us, and the debt to income ratio had gotten too high. He couldn't just quit and neither could I. By early in 2010, he confessed he was actively looking for something else because of a growing discord in our relationship (due to travel) and the weeks away from me and the kids were obviously not good for the family. I had agreed that this was the case, but in reality, we both knew that he would be in the tower climbing business for a while yet. So work continued...

Bridgette and the Hunny Bunn

Despite work and responsibilities, we had free-for-all-fun with one another. I had **the most fun** with Jonce (my nickname for him was Hunny Bunn). Sweet, sexy, funny, caring, attentive, and over-the-top handsome, my little redheaded fireball (seriously, pictures in the book... *handsome* man I tell you). We went to races, motorcycle rallies, parties, friend's cookouts, more rallies, more races, Alabama football games (Jonce was a **RABID** fan), and just about every other event one could imagine. We enjoyed, not just the events, but we enjoyed one another. We, as my father later pointed out, "crammed a lifetime of love and adventure into seven short years."

Jonce had the most contagious laugh. He belly laughed, turned red, and his whole body rocked when he was genuinely tickled by something. I have a Facebook video of that laugh that a dear friend sent to me after his death. I watch it regularly, to remember one of the things I loved most about him - his ability to laugh at almost anything. He also had an uncanny ability to get me to lighten up when I was entirely too serious. I could write an entire book about what I loved about Jonce, but this was one of the most vibrant things about him. His laugh could draw people in and hold them there. He was, in a word, magnetic.

I joked with the chapter title as you could plainly see, but I must say, more often than not, my marriage was blissful. Sure, we had marital woes to contend with, but all-in-all, our marriage was full of two-way love and adoration. Despite any setbacks, woes, misunderstandings, or fights that ensued during those almost four years of marriage, I can honestly say without reservation, that I did marry my best friend and I cannot wait until I am able to see him again and place my arms around him one more time.

5

HILDREN...

BEFORE AND AFTER MARRIAGE

Socializing

Daniel moved in before we wed, so I never got that "cutesy, honeymoon, can't get enough of each other marital bliss" married period. I loved being married. Loved it. Granted, I worried because we never had this "just hubby and wife" period at the onset of our marriage. I feared that by the time the children were grown and moved out (assuming they didn't try to move back home), we wouldn't know each other anymore, or worse, we might not like each other anymore. Hey, it happens.

Now in my opinion, a woman can feel several different ways about being married; 1) there is another child in the house, 2) blissful and content, 3) wishing she had poked her own eyes out with a fork, or 4) wishing she were in a padded room collecting her own drool into a paper cup. Most days, I fell somewhere between 1 and 3. For a long stretches, I maintained at 2, and only once had I felt number 4. With the help of the Pfizer Corporation, phase 4 did not last long. In my defense, I was defending my thesis and caring for the house and its members simultaneously, so Jonce really wasn't to blame. It was

59

mostly me. I have determined that marriage is a work of abstract art. Sometimes I don't "get it," but there is a beauty to it that I cannot deny.

Now, while I am not a ray of sunshine and light, I am by no means a full-on nag either. I liken myself to a tornado. They aren't an everyday occurrence, you never know when the storm may strike, it's usually fast, furious, short lived, and they leave a nasty zone of destruction. Oddly, the calm after the storm is eerie but oddly comforting. I think the differences between us in our marriage complimented one another, and our relationship was one of give and take. More take some days on his part, some on mine. Jonce was that beautiful social butterfly that could socialize for *days* on end. I'm not wired like that. When we met, we lived a state apart and we spent every other weekend together, so I only had to go out and socialize every other weekend at best. I didn't realize that "socializing" and "hanging out with friends" was going to be a weekly event. When I would visit during the courting process, I thought, "Surely to goodness, he just goes out this much because he wants to introduce me to people." I should have confirmed this assumption. Even after being married, going to just visit his family was an all-day (and into the next) social event for something as simple as a child's birthday party.

Hours, days, heck, even for weeks straight, I think the man could live in a highly charged social environment. He had no issues with loud music, confined spaces, seven different conversations, and screaming children all in one location for unspeakable stretches of time. During the first year living together, I convinced myself I was abnormal, entirely too tense, and probably a little too fussy. I mean, no one else at these events had near-death panic attacks in large gatherings, no one else would lock themselves in the bathroom and sit on the commode and rock and chant themselves into social submission.

Certainly, no one else in this group was ready to "accidentally" whoop people upside the head with a whiffle ball bat. Nope, just me. Thank goodness for Jonce, he was my rock most of the time. Eventually, I assimilated (or accommodated, whichever you prefer) and could hang with the best social crowd. Unfortunately, my inability to express that I didn't want to socialize 24/7 led us down a path where respect (for both of us) flew out the window, and my fussiness and impatience increased. This spiraled us into periods of not liking one another very much. Sad but true. In addition, I think the amount we socialized with friends also directly influenced our attitudes toward parenting and the manner in which we practiced our parenting skills.

Step Parenting Pitfalls

While I loved being married, but it was not without trials and tribulations in the first three years. Some of the stuff that had occurred had fractured the bond and the trust between us, and I have often found myself questioning exactly what I had gotten myself into. Now, I know that the main reason there were so many issues (and this is the beauty of hindsight) is that God was not the center of our marriage. I know with every fiber in my being that things could have been so much different, especially the manner in which we both handled parenting. Obviously, I was a little late in coming to this realization, but it gives me perspective for any future relationships. Before I continue into this chapter, let me make clear these are reflections based on my personal experience, perceptions, and feelings. I obviously would not want anything to be perceived as disrespectful.

To quote a relative of Jonce's "Sometimes parenting is like beating your head against a wooden wall and right when you think you have a breakthrough, you find out there is a cement wall right behind the wood one!" If you don't have God, it's more like steel, not cement. In my defense, I tried the best I knew how, but at several points, I relented all parenting responsibilities to my husband. During that point in my life, I felt like the only parent in the house and it felt overwhelming.

Biologically, these *were not my* children. In the infinite wisdom of my one friend, my job in this was to love and guide the children, not to raise them. This is presumably, why they have natural parents. While this is good in theory, sometimes doesn't actually play out like that, especially when one natural parent has tumultuous feelings toward the child's other natural parent. I tried to be loving, sweet, understanding, and patient. However, I am not at all ashamed to admit, I did not always handle things well. I was often over sensitive, I yelled too often, and my expectations were sometimes too high, given that a couple of the children had lacked structure almost all of their lives. I got to a point where I asked myself, "Bridgette, how long are you supposed to try? I mean if you are just going to be continually smacked in the head for it, what's the point?" I had limits, and I got dangerously close to reaching those limits more than once.

In addition, the stress I had at just being in the same room with one or more of the children really made me feel like a horrible wife and stepmother. I often found myself feeling I wanted a life free from children and the responsibility that goes with parenting. I am sure they noticed this and it is a demon I battled poorly. I realized I needed to either make more of an effort or get out. I knew in my heart that leaving was not the right answer, thus, my response was to place the parenting back on Jonce. I placed myself in "timeout" to regroup. I continue to find it ironic that as a social worker, I had no problems giving and encouraging the correct behavior to other parents, but I couldn't seem to manage executing them for my family's own benefit.

During the time before we married, two of the kids lived with us, and at the time, I don't think either one of them would have batted an eyelash in throwing me directly into heavy traffic. To be most accommodating, to you, my reader, let's take this kid by kid.

Daniel

The period after Daniel moved in, but before Becky arrived, was particularly difficult for me. I felt I had been thrown headlong into this parenting thing, and had no clue what I was doing. On top of that, Daniel is a... HE. It appeared I was always messing up whatever it was that I actually tried to do. I was accommodating, I helped with homework, I went to a little league football game or two, I tried to "talk" to him, and I "grounded" him when that didn't work. I tried every trick in my bag. Apparently, that wasn't enough. I encountered a dirty bedroom, foul language (he didn't always know I heard it), damage to our property, destruction of my personal articles, writing on and smearing gum on walls, and an attitude that occasionally left much to be desired.

Most painful, was the destruction of something my late mother had given me. Granted, it was just one of two comforters my mother had bought me, but it had great sentimental value. We had bought the comforters during a trip when she felt particularly good after a radiation treatment. To have your step child take a ball point ink pen and write the word "HATE" on it... ughghgh! It raises my blood pressure even now. It wasn't that he didn't know his anger could have been handled a different way, he did it on purpose to get to me. It was nasty, hateful, and there was no excuse in my opinion. Jonce tried to discipline him, but I think his resentment towards me was just too much for Daniel.

After Becky moved in, I sensed that Daniel felt a little more empowered and brazen. Now with a younger sister in tow, he had someone to blame, someone to enlist in driving me crazy when Jonce wasn't around, and someone to "show out" in front of. Thus, I felt he set the tone for Becky's role when he later left our home. Together, I would have preferred to wrestle two cats into a bathtub. Daniel and Becky, who having been raised mostly by extended family or their natural mother, were not accustomed to our structure or discipline. To boot, I know my tone, short fuse, and impatience did not help matters.

Daniel was not particularly used to having boundaries. Thus, when the living arrangements changed, the line in the sand had to be drawn, and it was much closer than he suspected. It wasn't an endless beach anymore; it was more like a sandbox. In our home, there were rules, boundaries, expectations, and discipline for crossing that line.

When things got tough, when things were expected, when discipline was exacted, he wanted to get going…right back to grandmas. We did the revolving door a few times, and in the end, decided he was of the age, and he could make his own decision. We tried to instill in him that when things were hard, you needed to dig in and work it out. We told him the last time he had come back to live with us, "Daniel, this is not a revolving door. You choose to go back to grandma, that's it; there is no coming back. We love you and don't want you to go, but this back and forth is not an option. You either stay and work it out, or live with grandma and live with the consequences of that."

He chose the latter. Jonce and I both wished that he hadn't. The event that led up to his leaving was an incident in the utility room before school. We were already late for school, I had an appointment, and he had not done something before leaving the home that he was supposed to do. I told him to come back in the house and get it done so we could go. He stomped back in the house, and took care of the chore. He then huffed, puffed, and bowed up at me before going back to the car (something he had done once previously already). I *will not, and I mean I will not tolerate an act of aggression in my home by a child.* I kept my cool, but not the nicest of terms, I told him to get his rear end back in the car. After school, when I went to pick him up, he refused to come home.

I know some people may feel as though we kicked him out, or we abandoned him. We did not. I wasn't prepared to be a parent as it was, and when that is coupled with an increase in attitude and anger, things can easily go from bad to worse. Daniel did not seem to understand that he had to share people in his life (father, grandfather, grandmother) with other people, and (in my opinion) when those relationships felt threatened, he lashed out. Right or wrong, the relationship with both his father and me became better with him living with his grandparents.

Becky

Having a twelve-year-old boy was more than I was ready for. Having a ten-year-old girl move in, at first, was a relief. I thought, "Well, whew! I used to be a ten-year-old girl, I can hang. I *can do* this." What I had totally overlooked (or thought would be no big deal) was the life from which she came, and the influence that her brother would have on her once she moved into our home. Naively, I thought having a sibling around would occupy them, make them close, make the attitudes level out. It did not have this effect. Let me provide you, the reader, with some imagery to accurately describe *my perception* of things at the time.

> Now, if you would be so kind, please look to the left of your chair where you are reading. There should be several large, thick cut pork chops. Now, tie them to my neck. After this is accomplished, open up the front door, and you should see two mastodon-sized pit bulls. Hurl me out the door.

This was my mentality within a month after Becky had moved in. At least for the first two years, I excused many behaviors from Becky, as did Jonce. Becky, while living with her grandmother and mother, had a difficult childhood. Yes, Jonce should have gotten her sooner, he should have moved her away, and provided her a home away from her mother. Why this never happened, I still am not completely sure, other than he wasn't able to or was too afraid to raise her alone. Jonce admitted to me (more than once) that he felt like he was not a good parent for a long time, and had been entirely too selfish.

We *both* excused behaviors with the reasoning, "look at the turmoil she had with her mom and the death of her grandmother." I did it too. I excused and excused, and excused. That approach got us nowhere fast. I gave some serious leeway, but after a year to a year and a half of living in our home, she knew what was expected in our home, she knew right from wrong, and she knew what was acceptable. This "reasoning" of how she had been raised went from being a reason to being an excuse. I got to a point where I felt like I couldn't tolerate it anymore.

From the beginning, she was angry that we took her from her mother and was probably somewhat confused, although we tried our best to explain. In our best efforts, we allowed contact with her mother and her side of the family. Much to our detriment, I feel that this, in combination with my ineptitudes, and Jonce's lack of early involvement, created the situation we had at the time. Had our family and marriage been God-Centered, I believe we could have combated this more efficiently.

Before Jonce's death, we dealt with typical child/teenage behaviors from Becky that were to be expected and a few I thought were over the top. Sometimes I wondered if what I perceived was motivated by a loathing for me personally (the sister comforter to the one that Daniel had destroyed had been the object of *her* destruction). Taken separately, these behaviors could have been manageable, but together, had driven me almost to the point of divorce. Becky and I had periods of getting along and then periods of worsening behaviors on her part and ill-equipped parenting, poor attitude, and fear on my part. My poor parenting skills, "gunny sacking" of anger, and Jonce's lack of previous parenting had driven us to couples counseling.

I told him, "we go to counseling, or I pack my bags." He told me that we would do whatever we needed to do. He told me, "I married you for forever, and we are going to fix it. Whatever it takes." This was actually about six months before his death.

Michael

Michael, I once believed was the most well-adjusted of my stepchildren. I attributed this mostly to the fact that his mother (Jonce's first wife) is a well-oiled, maternal machine of parental love and patience. She had gone "overboard" according to Michael, but from my perspective, her patience seems endless. She is a woman of God. Coincidence? I think not.

This child, and the fact he was raised by two parents, is the rationale for why he and I got along better than the others did. About halfway through his final year of high school, he decided that he wanted to come live with his dad. I decided that this could in fact be a wonderful thing. A responsible teenage boy, nearing early adulthood, could provide an influence to Daniel and Becky (Daniel hadn't moved out yet).

I missed the mark, but only slightly. I thought he wanted to move in to bond with his brother, sister, and father before entering the abyss of adulthood. No, what he wanted was to run wild, and I am not sure he was even aware of the definition of responsibility. After moving in, he finished his senior year, could not or would not hold a job, slept all day, and partied until untold hours. All the while, these activities were generously overlooked by his father. The "boys will be boys" syndrome appeared to reign supreme, and Jonce swore it was just Michael letting off steam. Michael had lived with his mother and stepfather up until this point, and I felt that Jonce tried to alleviate his own guilt for not being in Michael's life much before this point. Jonce did later admit to me that this assessment was in fact correct.

I take full responsibility for setting a poor example myself in some instances. For instance, Jonce and I might have drunk alcoholic beverages, but we shouldn't have been drinking in front of the children. Jonce and I would have family and friends over …A LOT…and alcohol consumption was the norm. If we did not want Michael to drink, we should not have created the environment. I mean, it wasn't a house of ill repute for crying out loud, but still, we both could have made better choices.

I still feel a shudder in my spine at the rationalization from Jonce, "I was *so* much worse when I was his age." I complained, I moaned, and I made my point that just because he sometimes behaved poorly or made bad choices when he was young, did not excuse bad behavior from the children. I eventually gave up making this point, because I felt that Jonce wasn't hearing me. I should not have just let it go. These issues have been addressed much sooner, that was *my* fault. Instead, I seethed internally and let it build. Mount Vesuvius had nothing on me, I assure you.

After about a year out of high school, Michael worked intermittently and spent most of his time with his girlfriend. While I cannot attest to the time when Michael realized that he had to propel forward into adulthood, I can say he did so vigorously. In part due to the guidance of his father, Michael chose to enlist in the United States Air Force (Praise God). While some parents and stepparents may be worried about such a decision, given world affairs, I thought this was the most mature decision he had ever made.

Brad

I don't know where to begin. All his life, according to my husband, and later according to Brad himself, his mother had choice words regarding Jonce. According to Brad, it was only recently before Jonce's death, that he had told his mother, stepfather, and extended family that he was going to see his father and spend time with Jonce, regardless of whatever they had to say about him.

Brad told Jonce and me about the things she had told Brad about Jonce. Brad said he felt those things were contradictory from the person Brad knew Jonce to be. During the six plus years I had been with Jonce, I had seen Brad in as many times as I have fingers on one hand. Since his father's death, Brad still calls, and comes around sporadically to check on me and to visit.

∽༖∽

Jonce had been a stepfather in his third marriage, but had no children with said third wife, Tonya. Donny, Tim, and Ann were Tonya's children from a previous marriage and according to Jonce, and his entire family, Tim and Donny were a "handful." Both boys had been in some trouble here and there while Tonya and Jonce were married. During our courtship, both boys came to Jonce to make amends for the tribulations they put him through all those years ago. It was not until they had aged, and had the distance and experience of life to understand that he had done what he saw was best for them at the time. Ann is smart, funny, polite, caring, considerate, and fully aware of the blessing Jonce was in her life.

It is this situation, which Jonce was particularly fond of using as his frame of reference to assist me my attempts at child rearing. I felt that Jonce continually hurled that boulder of "When I was a stepparent, I..." towards me when he disagreed with something I did or didn't do. While I appreciate the experience and wisdom he acquired during his marriage to Tonya, it still felt to me that I was being chastised. In addition, all the children are different creatures entirely. Ultimately, Jonce and Tonya divorced, so I guess I never really heeded any advice of his well-intentioned advice.

Jonce and I, in our third year of marriage, discussed the shortcomings of __our__ parenting experiences. He would have been the first to tell you that he had always relied much too heavily on the women he was married to or "with" to help him raise his children. I readily admitted to not being patient and a temper that occasionally got the better of me. In short, we both admitted that we had major flaws and that things needed fixing.

Counseling was a wonderful experience, and things were getting so much better before he was tragically taken. Our therapist was fabulous. I even continued to see her after Jonce passed away. She listened to us moan and complain, and was always ready to encourage, support, and prod where needed. She had an uncanny ability to make us find our own answers (individually and as a couple) without making us feel stupid or inept. Counselors and therapists are a professional breed like no other.

Relationships Now...

I suppose I adjusted to the "parenting thing," but not to the degree I wanted to before Jonce passed away. After his death, Becky remained with me about a year. However, she now lives with Jonce's father and stepmother. She appears to be doing well and we talk occasionally. Daniel remains stoic and does not talk to me unless we cross paths. When we do speak, he is sweet, polite, and cordial. I worry about him though.

Michael is in a committed relationship and has had a child since Jonce's death. I am still friends with Jonce's first wife (Michael's mom), and the only thing I can say is that while I am hopeful of what's to come for him, both his mother and I still worry that he isn't completely on track. I think it's just a woman's nature to worry about her kids [step kids]. In the interim, all her and I are able to do is pray for Michael, his girlfriend (soon to be wife, last I heard), and the baby.

Brad peeks out now and again to talk to me or ask how I am doing. I don't speak to him unless he calls or visits. He is with someone who has three kids, and appears to be doing well. He still contends he wants to enlist in the Marines just like his dad. I hope that he does, and if he does, I know Jonce would be proud.

Jonce and I both had histories of being active in church and being brought up in the Christian faith, even though we weren't consistent in going to church and following Christ the way we should have. Both of us had been saved and if I am going to be brutally honest here, I knew better, and so did Jonce. We should have made efforts to attend church, been better examples, live our lives as God would have had us live them, but we didn't. I regret that periodically since losing him, but I know I am not perfect and I make mistakes. I also know God is a forgiving God and that because I ask in earnest, I am forgiven for the mistakes I made on purpose or by omission. I have been given His Grace and the ability to start again.

Two verses that strike me, as far as my parental shortcomings are:

Proverbs 22:6, "Train up a child in the way he should go; even when he is old he will not depart from it. (NIV)

Philippians 3:12-13, "I don't mean to say that I have already achieved these things or that I have already reached perfection. But I press on to possess that perfection for which Christ Jesus first possessed me. No, dear brothers and sisters, I have not achieved it, but I focus on this one thing: Forgetting the past and looking forward to what lies ahead." (NIV)

I honestly believe that had Jonce and I did what was expected of us, had been more mindful of our responsibilities, and were more patient as parents, the family unit would have had more harmony, and the bonds forged might have been closer. I have often recited worries in my mind such as "If I had just gotten him to go to church," "If I had been more adamant about going to church," "If I had...," "If Jonce had..."

I think any well-(semi) adjusted person can agree that that's not healthy, and it's not an effective way to contend with grief. God knew everything. He knew our shortcomings, our stupid decisions as parents, what we were or were not doing right, the time and date of Jonce's death, the path that would lead me down, and the path that the children would take with their lives after his death. This is one of those "God's the one in control" moments. I realized I really just had to "let it go," because God's "got this."

6

MARITAL WOES...

As I said earlier, the marriage "fairy tale" does not exist. *All* marriages have trials and tribulations. If marriages didn't have their difficulties, we would never be able to fully appreciate the beauty of marriage, or the beauty of our spouses. I stopped writing this book for a few weeks wondering how I would approach this. I want you to have a full, healthy picture of not only my husband, but of me, and the family as a whole. Without dragging things on forever, my goal was, at this point, for you to be able to feel how much I loved and adored my husband. I wanted you to see and feel how the elements in our lives, both before and after we met, shaped us.

Overall, I considered (and still do) my marriage to have been a strong and happy one, with many happy and loving times and adventures. However, that does not negate the trials, fights, and literally torturous periods that tossed us around like the proverbial ship at sea. Having said that, I question my level of personal disclosure here. Mainly I want to convey important things that I wrestled with after his death, but I don't think airing every single piece of dirty laundry is honoring God or my late husband. Therefore, I will attempt honesty with modesty. I realize some people are going to assume things. Some might ponder what I am "really trying to say," and I can't help that. What I can help is being faithful in what I know to be true about my husband, my marriage, and myself to him.

All married couples struggle in one or more areas - employment, [dis] respect, violence, alcohol or substance abuse, poor parenting, indifference, infidelity, nagging, mental and emotional turmoil, just to name a few. Jonce and I were lovers, best friends, each other's biggest supporters, and harshest critic. While we struggled in some areas, both of us had a huge fault when it came to dealing with marital matters. Both of us had a genuine knack for becoming bull-headed, *blindly* opinionated, and, at times, selfish, hateful, and unforgiving. I was a "gunny sacker" and Jonce was a "yeller." It made for some interesting and painful fights.

In some respects, Jonce and I were not different from any other couple. Life gets busy, it gets hard, pressures mount, and explosions and arguments happen. We are human, and it is to be expected. In tiptoeing around one another to avoid an argument, we occasionally found ourselves knee deep in landmines. This is obviously not enjoyable and completely it's avoidable. Communication is the key factor in a marriage, and I see that now more than I ever have before. If I had learned to express myself more clearly without reverting to the ice queen treatment, and he could have communicated without being so easily frustrated and irritated with me, we might have gotten further.

Every area, and I mean EVERY AREA, of contention that we battled through could have had a much more productive outcome if the lines of communication had been maintained. Instead, more than once, one of us took wire cutters to the line. Hindsight is a wonderful thing, but it can make for a path filled with regret, grief, and guilt after the one you love most is gone.

Our marital areas of strife included, but were not limited to accusations of infidelity (on both parts), parenting (or lack thereof), finances, selfishness, drinking, my inverted behavior when angry, his loud behavior when angry, workaholic tendencies, inability to agree on returning to the church, and our extensive social life. Each area had its own hot buttons, and each created an anxiety in one or both of us. I know for me, I pushed buttons in him because I *knew* it would get him angry, I *knew* I would get a response, I *knew* if I got him angry enough he would listen to me. At least that's what I thought.

Yeah, that doesn't work so well. I finally learned that, and luckily, I learned it before he passed away. When he pushed my buttons, I think his intentions were more commendable than mine were. In fact, I think he fell over "trip lines" more than he intentionally pushed any of my buttons. Regardless of how we got there, when we did get there, it wasn't pretty.

One might have thought what I was after was getting an admission of some kind of guilt, an admission that I was right and he was wrong, or that I knew better than he did about some things. What did I really want? At the time, I am not sure I could have pinpointed what I was really after. In retrospect, I can say now that I wanted more connectedness, more intimacy, more of an actual partnership, especially where parenting was concerned. The whole "means to an end" thing warped my thinking. Ladies, when you insist, nag, pester, and mother your husband, or when you shut out or shut down, there are no "means" that will give you the "end" you seek.

I am not perfect, far from it, in fact. I am not who I was (Praise God!), but I am not yet who God intends me to be (Double Praise God!). I gladly, loudly, and openly declare my part in the things that made the rough patches in my marriage worse. I will own that because I caused it, and if by telling it, I can, at the very least, make my readers stop and think, then I don't care one little bit what anyone thinks. I was at times a harsh person to live with. I was testy, ill tempered, overbearing, and over accommodating. I am not saying I was a raving lunatic, but I will say that I could have handled my expressions more thoughtfully in tone, clarity, and delivery.

If I had changed the way that I argued or communicated, it might have saved tremendous amounts of strife. If the communication had been different, we could have avoided baseless allegations on both of our parts, periods of the silent treatment, worry, anxiety, sleepless nights, hurt feelings, and periods of both of us feeling unloved and disrespected. If Jonce had learned sooner to quiet his tone, and avoid communicating through actions that were hurtful or scary, I might have been more inclined to talk to him instead of shutting down and withdrawing into the bedroom. In response, we might have been able to communicate what we really wanted from one another. If anyone wants a book that explains the strife of poor communication on a marriage, then, I highly recommend "The Love and Respect Connection" by Emerson Eggerich (uplifting and quite the revelation). Suffice it to say, communication was our downfall.

As a final note, I want to pass along a small gem of wisdom that I learned through the marital woes that we faced. Counseling is a tool at your disposal not to ignore. Counselors are a special breed to serve those in need, especially within the body of Christ. One name that we know Jesus by is Wonderful Counselor *(Isaiah 9:6)*. Coincidence? I think not *(Proverbs 16:9)*. Having a third party that can listen objectively and sincerely attend to the issues within a marriage (pre, post, or even a relationship between significant others) is a special and rare gift given to people that, I feel, is a Godly calling of one's heart. What you have to ask yourself, and your spouse, is how hard are you willing to fight for your marriage? Are you willing to honor the vows that you took before Him?

I think a little brutal insight might be required here, and if getting mad at me makes you feel better, then so be it. I know not all marriages can be saved, and there are some marriages in which there is a biblical justification for divorce *(Matthew 5:32; 19:9)*. However, God commanded us within the confines of marriage for a man to unconditionally love his wife, and for a wife to unconditionally respect her husband *(Ephesians 5:33)*.

What you have to ask yourself is this: Are you willing to abandon what He has called you to do because you are too embarrassed or too selfish to try every available tool at your disposal? If your answer to this is yes, you don't only need to reevaluate your marriage, you need to reevaluate where your relationship is with the Lord. It is a humbling and often painful task to ask yourself the hard questions, but if you do not hold yourself accountable to God and your spouse, who will?

Jonce riding Blade in Memphis

Jonce & Bridgette St. Patrick's Day 2008

Ali and Barry Sloan

Jonce and I on our wedding day

Accident Site in Anniston after the accident 7/22/2010

Accident Site in Anniston after the accident 7/22/2010

Accident Site in Anniston after the accident 7/22/2010

PART TWO

LIFE AFTER DEATH

7

GODWINK

I sat out all day on the front porch, the morning following Jonce's death. I went in to get a drink and use the ladies' room, but overall, I just sat. After my eyes had become particularly puffy, I went into the house, retrieved a cool washrag to wipe my face, and marched back to the front porch. Shortly after, I think a friend came by to sit with me. While I was sitting there, a tiny, newly born, black and yellow monarch butterfly fluttered around on the porch and dive-bombed me for a moment or two. It then came to rest on my knee. Then it fluttered to my flip-flop, back to my knee, buzzed my head, and back to my knee and feet.

Quizzically, I looked and was completely astounded that this lil' guy wasn't leaving. I shook my leg, tapped my foot, got up, and sat back down. I became enchanted with it and made a comment to him.

"Look Jonce, you never liked my feet when you were here, what is your fascination this morning?"

I giggled, and then immediately started crying again. I had placed Jonce's identity on this butterfly. Even though I knew it wasn't possible for Jonce to be *in* the butterfly, it felt like he was there with me. It was like a little delicate piece of comfort and beauty despite the previous night's events. After I composed myself yet again and wiped my face, I lay the washcloth on my knee. A few flutters later, he landed on my washrag.

I picked the washrag up by a corner and let it dangle. I shook it, twirled it, and laid it back down on my knee, yet my little butterfly continued to stay. He tickled my knee as he walked, floated a few times around, but always stayed on me. I found myself smiling and then immediately feeling guilty for taking the slightest pleasure in anything, but I couldn't help myself. As best as my memory serves me, that little butterfly was around me and on me for the better part of an hour or two. I noticed later, that the butterfly only left after more people had arrived at my house.

Once the porch became active with people, the butterfly quietly went on his way. In retrospect, I know that God sent me a little piece of love, comfort, and beauty to amuse and delight me in my worst and darkest hour. Only when the loving and comforting arms of friends and family had arrived did the little butterfly leave. It was as if God had sent me this little piece of Himself to comfort and hold me until my family and friends could do it for Him. I had just been Godwinked.

8

$\mathcal{T}$HE CHASM AND THE

BRIDGE

Having been touched by what I now consider my own personal Godwink, the days leading up to the viewing and burial were more tolerable than they would have been otherwise. I camped out on our front porch the days following his death, up until the viewing and funeral. I don't mean I spent hours on the porch, I mean *days*. Bless my friends and family.

Our friend, Chad, brought me an industrial fan to place on the porch so that no one sweltered to death, and there I sat. It was the end of July, and the temperatures ranged anywhere from 95-100 degrees each day with humidity at 90+ percent. Anyone who came by was always welcome to go in the house and mill around, sit, talk, and visit with one another, but my porch and my front table were my refuge. The butterflies seemed constant in my alone moments and fluttered by through the yard when people were at the house.

Planning, orchestrating, and living through the time up to the funeral of your spouse are no small feats. It's a chasm of sorts; a wide divide between realizing the loss you are enduring and being able to attach some modicum of finality. ***Not closure... finality***. This chasm, if you allow it, will stretch out so far it looks like an insurmountable ravine. Fortunately, God places people in your path who create a human bridge. Arms, hearts, kisses, hugs, sorrowful expressions of wanting to take your pain, homemade casseroles, and an endless supply of pure humanity. All of these elements in the human spirit interlock with you and one another to guide you safely to the other side. When you cross over, you are simultaneously tired, depressed, appreciative, and joyous for the love you have been given. In a word - astounding.

In the days directly after Jonce's death, my best friend, Heather, and my entire family arrived in force. Heather's mere presence was one of the most comforting to me. She was the one who kept me from losing it completely. We are not blood sisters, but I would give my life for her. She astounds me with her sweet heart and spirit. I hope I am to her a fraction of the friend she has been and is to me.

During the time I spent with family and friends leading up to the funeral, I was consumed by tasks - flower choices, a casket, the burial plot, headstone decisions, hiring a lawyer to retain custody of Becky and to handle the legalities of what had happened to Jonce, and other such tasks. Praise God for Andray, my father-in-law. Andray handled all of the church arrangements, helped me pick out the casket and other necessities, and Jonce's grandfather handled Jonce's resting place. Andray wanted the funeral at his home church, The Church of Christ in Guntersville, to which I readily agreed.

Jonce and I had arguments back and forth over the last year or two about going to church. We took Becky regularly, dropped her off at the local church she wanted to attend, or friends picked her up and dropped her off. Jonce had reservations about being a hypocrite, and I never pushed the issue. We didn't have a church to call our own, so I was so relieved and happy at Andray's suggestion.

The church was booked for one thing or another on Sunday, so the viewing was actually held on that Monday, July 26, 2010 and the funeral July 27, 2010. To add salt to the family's wounds, the 26th is Andray's birthday and the 27th is Jason's (Jonce's brother) birthday. There was really no way around this for us, but it was horrible to have to watch them bear having the viewing and funeral on their birthdays.

Through all this arranging, decision-making, weeping, screaming, insomnia, and lack of appetite, I was truly blessed with a myriad of friends and family that maintained my household, and helped take care of Becky. I was, as we say in the South, "petted on," "loved on," and my "heart blessed" until I thought my heart might burst. The love and devotion of my work family from the Department of Human Resources overwhelms me to tears even now. I received thousands of messages on Facebook, and received as many text messages and phone calls. I am not exaggerating here. I noticed later on the phone bill that in the weeks following Jonce's death, I had received and sent well over **10,000** text messages and hundreds of phone calls. The only description I have for these days immediately after his death and up until the funeral is abounding love and comfort.

In this chasm between July 22nd and July 27th, I was kept busy by a flurry of activity between inquiring with lawyer friends and talking with Becky about her custody. Becky's mother was *not* an option, so it was either her grandparents or me. Ultimately, Becky decided that she wanted to live with me. That was all I needed to hear. As soon as the funeral was over, I filed paperwork. I also tried to keep the house going, but my friends and family shooed me away from cleaning, chores, laundry, cooking, and other mundane things so I could concentrate on the funeral and getting to see Alison Sloan.

Alison was not only my friend, but also the widow of the other man who died on the scene of the accident. I needed to see her at least once before Jonce's funeral. In the midst of my own pain and grief, I never lost sight of Alison. Barry Sloan was the other worker on the tower with Jonce. In the blink of an eye, Alison went from being the one time intern at the Department of Human Resources to my *sister*. Barry was originally from Mississippi and so the funeral and the burial for Barry would take place there. In the interim, Alison held a memorial service in Guntersville for Barry. Because Jonce's arrangements had been delayed due to the church being utilized, this afforded me the opportunity to have the time to see Alison and pay my respects: God's providence (*Philippians 4:19 NIV*).

Our hometown of Guntersville is small, tight, and very connected. Barry and Jonce's deaths were on the tongues of the town's citizens within a few hours of the accident. A "city in mourning" is the only accurate description I have. I believe Barry's memorial was Sunday July 25, 2010. I had managed to get out of the house to get a black dress that was comfortable in the summer heat, and made my way to the memorial.

By this time, everyone knew that I was "the other widow" and the longer I stayed at the funeral home, the more people were approaching me to give their condolences. I realized how thoughtful and heartfelt they were, but I left almost immediately because I felt like it was taking away from the purpose of the moment: to remember Barry and to comfort Alison. I told her I loved her, and told her why I was leaving. We embraced, told each other we loved one another, and promised to call one another in a few days upon her return from Barry's funeral.

After returning home, I alternated between piddling around the house, and sitting on the porch. I smoked cigarettes, drank coffee in the mornings, and beer as the day progressed. Most of our friends were drinkers and came to visit with a cooler in tow. Jonce's love of beer and socialization made it all seemed kosher and appropriate. We would all raise a toast and relive everyone's most treasured memories. Friends and family brought food, cleaning supplies, toilet paper, paper towels, and an endless supply of whatever else I needed, even if I didn't know I needed it. My particularly favorite memory of this horrible time in my life is that of "my girls" from the office. Gracie, Valerie, Emily, Keesha, and several others came and presented me the three essential food groups in those days, nicotine, coffee, and chocolate. They *know* me.

I found that I was allowing myself a small giggle or intermittent smile during those days leading up to the funeral. My friends were (and are) amazing, and they took every opportunity they could to make me smile or laugh with a memory of Jonce. I took comfort in the fact that although Jonce was not with us any longer, it was evident through their stories just how much he was loved, adored, and cherished by his friends and family.

My last and most personal act I did for Jonce before the viewing had to be completed before the viewing. His father and I drove to the funeral home to check if things were "acceptable" to us, to see if he looked the "way that would be most fitting." One of the hardest things I have ever done is walking through those doors and seeing my husband lying in a box. I silently and subconsciously gave thanks for the preceding days and the flurry of friends and family that had been by my side. If they had not been there, supporting and loving me, making me laugh occasionally, and forcing at least a mild amount of nutrition into me, I wouldn't have been able to handle this final task.

Jonce looked so handsome. He was in his brother's Marine Dress Blues. Jonce had sold his after getting out of the service (a fact that he regretted and lamented about more than once during our life together). Spit polished and shined, he looked so strikingly handsome that it took my breath.

The injuries that he sustained were severe and the official cause of death was "blunt force trauma," thus there was the use of heavy makeup and, what I can only assume to be, artificial limbs for his left arm and right leg below the knee. Although *I* could see the bruises and the small changes in the fabric where I knew things were missing, I knew that the funeral home staff had taken extraordinary care to honor my husband. I remember looking at him and smiling a little. I made a comment on how handsome he was. My eyes swelled, and my heart broke all over again. I, however, had a job to do.

Our friends and I can tell you hysterical stories about the great care Jonce took in styling his hair and preparing his clothes. I often joked with him that he was the woman in the relationship when it came to preparing to leave the house. I can get dressed in fifteen minutes flat. That's shower, hair, make up, and dress. Often I was resigned to watching TV or reading a book waiting on Jonce to ready himself for presentation.

I sucked it up, and proceeded to do the task for which I had come. I looked at Jimmy, the funeral home director, thanked him, and then proceeded to whip out the hair gel and pomade. My husband, bless his heart, was anally retentive about his appearance, and he <u>*WAS NOT*</u> being laid to eternal rest until I had beaten down that cowlick and ensured that every hair was in place. Oddly, Jonce used to have a complete (as we Southerners say) "come apart" if I so much as came within three feet of his hair. The irony was not lost on me, but that cowlick was being tamed, and I wasn't leaving until it had.

No one tells you how *absolutely cold* and hard a body is in death. Even if someone had warned me, I wouldn't have been prepared. Until you have experienced it, there are no human words to define the experience. It is a surreal, disconcerting feeling, and it is *very very* final. When I started fixing his hair, the sensation really took me aback. Most people probably won't talk about this, but I will. I realized later that this was an important event in my healing process.

As I traveled down this road of healing, I realized something. On the one hand, touching him gave me a sense of deep sadness and grief, on the other hand, I took immense comfort in the fact that I ... **I**, was the last one to lovingly provide an act of service for him before he was laid to rest. However, I also became keenly aware that the man I loved, cherished, and respected wasn't there anymore. It solidified for me the indisputable fact that he had passed away and had gone to be with God. Beforehand, the knowledge of that was in the abstract. After tending to this seemingly small and menial task, I realized there was nothing abstract about it. To this day, trying to fix his hair is one of the most intimate and special moments in my heart following his death. Despite the shock, discomfort, and the sadness it caused me, I wouldn't trade it for anything in this world.

After about three minutes, with a grimace of frustration and tear-filled eyes, I turned to Jimmy

"Do you have like concrete hairspray or *something* that will hold this in place?"

"I absolutely do, I will be right back."

Five minutes, a few choice words to Jonce about his hair, and a few more intense choice words spoken directly to the cowlick, his hair was ready. I am sure Jonce would have done much better, but I was also keenly aware that Jonce would be able to appreciate how incredibly difficult it was for me to do, and he would have commended me on a job well done.

9

THE MEASURE OF A MAN

The Viewing

I have always heard the saying that "The measure of a man is evident in what he accomplishes and what he leaves behind, but the *true* measure of a man is how much he is missed when he leaves this earth." Who should get original credit for this, I have no idea, but there are words no more apt than these are when it comes to Jonce Hubble.

First, being a member of the Southern Cruisers Riding Club is being a member of an external family, which numbers in the hundreds. News of Jonce's death spread like wildfire through the SCRC family and the outpouring was nothing short of incredible. Bikers came from all over the country to pay homage to their fellow biker, their friend, and their brother. I continuously received emails and Facebook messages in the days following his death. Bikers from all over the United States (and even overseas), lamented and apologized about not being able to attend Jonce's viewing or funeral.

At the viewing, the SCRC assembled the Biker Guard. These men and women stood at attention with SCRC and American flags around the church lawn and walkways. Stoic faced and facing forward in 95-degree weather, they never moved, their attention never faltered, and their eyes remained forward. It was the most touching tribute from the SCRC I had ever witnessed. My understanding is that this is customary for the SCRC at funerals of fallen bikers; I just had never had the privilege of seeing it for myself.

Guests, who paid their respects at the viewing and the funeral, were told to feel free to dress up, wear casual dress, dress in riding gear, and/or dress in Alabama Football attire. The best estimate the funeral director (and my friend) and I were able to determine from the viewing and the funeral combined was close to *one thousand* people. I spent most of the viewing in and out of the church greeting and hugging people, thanking them for coming. Customarily, I suppose the widow is supposed to remain in the church the entire viewing, but I didn't feel that I could. My daddy told me to do what I wanted to do and what I felt I needed to do.

So, I walked, hugged, kissed, and thanked everyone. How could I sit in the church with a line of people outside? For crying out loud, the church could easily hold 500 people, and it was full. There was a line of people from the door to the far left side of the building, waiting to say goodbye. Every one of them needed to know I appreciated them for coming and for loving my husband. I would not plant my rear end in the church and cry myself into oblivion. I had been doing that for days so far, and I was certain I would be for years to come. I remembered that viewings are often sad at the start, but as they progress, the more people will smile, laugh, and tell stories about the one who has passed. This makes the viewing more bittersweet than miserable. This viewing was no exception.

Being among friends and family, who had come to bid him farewell, seemed to lighten the pain and remind me that death is not an end, but a beginning, a homecoming. I was, and continue to be, forever grateful that Jonce had been saved earlier in his life. I knew that, in the coming months and years, I wouldn't have to worry about whether or not I would see Jonce again. For years, he had been saved, he had gone to church, but had only stopped in recent years for various reasons. In my earlier years, I too was raised in church and saved. I knew I would see him again, and that he would recognize me once I got to Heaven.

The Funeral

I got to the church a little early and stood outside, so that I could see Bill "Jarhead" Strebel, an SCRC brother, drive Jonce's motorcycle to the church. That was probably the most torturous moment - to see that bike with someone else on it. At the same time, it was the sweetest, most tender moment of the day for me as well. Jarhead is an amazing man and loved Jonce as a brother. Having him ride "Blade" (this was the bike's name) could not have been more beautiful or fitting.

The actual funeral was more difficult than I could possibly begin to explain. Walking down the aisle of the church toward the casket of your deceased spouse is an experience I would not wish on my worst enemy. There was a surreal, light-headed moment where I thought I might actually crumple to the ground. Fortunately, I made it to my seat in front and sat through the funeral in a fog. I am not sure who said what or who spoke the eulogy (I believe it was a former pastor of Andray's). Many people from the viewing were unable to attend the funeral itself, but the church was still full. Their love and support kept me from falling apart.

I don't know the exact number of people who attended, but I remember about a quarter of the congregation dressed in leather. Even in your darkest moments, that much leather tends to stand out as a vivid memory. Bikers occupied the right front pew section for probably the depth of fifteen pews. That is a lot of bikers, and a "whole lot of love." Family and friends crowded pews through the rest of the church - and then there was Wanda.

I love my friend. She photographed Jonce's funeral and viewing for the family. I had one requirement. DO. NOT. TAKE. A. PICTURE. OF. JONCE. IN. THAT. BOX.... DO. NOT. I had seen this done in the past at other funerals. I don't like it. It creeps me out and it's morbid. Wanda, the true friend she is followed instructions to the "T." She later recounted that she accidently got one of the casket and noticed there was a tiny part where you could see Jonce. I couldn't really tell from the picture, and besides that, Wanda had issues trying to take pictures because her body was shaking with sobs the whole time. God Bless Wanda Tillman Williams.

In her grief, she did this for me and I will cherish that act of love and remembrance the rest of my days. True friendship (at least to me) is when you put aside your own hurt, pain, or feelings (regardless of the situation) and plow forward for your friends. I don't care if it makes you angry, sad, or uncomfortable. You stand by your friends, no matter what. Period. Wanda is the epitome of this. She is the "Apple of my Pie."

I spoke at Jonce's funeral to the congregation. I barely remember what I said, but I am glad I did so. Oddly enough, as far as funerals go, Jonce's had been one of the most comforting I have ever experienced. I also remember greeting *EVERY* person in the congregation at the side of the casket during the service. I thought later that this might have been a bit much for people, or that I had drug out the process. However, as my daddy said, this is *your* husband's funeral, do what you need to do. So I did. I thought it was important for me to hug or shake hands with every person in the room. They gave of their time, energy, and love to support us in our darkest hour. I was going to make certain that they knew I knew that.

In addition, I could hear Jonce in my ear the whole time, "MY GOSH! This many people turned out to see me off!? Really!? WOW. This is humbling but very cool. Bridgette, you better make sure you thank *every person in this room.*" I am certain that I would have regretted not doing this, and I didn't want to disappoint Jonce, not even in death.

⊱⊰

After everyone had said goodbye, the family remained in the sanctuary. Personally, I needed to see the casket close. I can't really explain it. For most people, I guess, watching their loved one actually be interred in the cemetery is the moment of finality. For me personally, it was the lock of the casket, the final goodbye, my last whisper. I knew that would set the finality in place for me. I knew I didn't want to watch the casket be lowered as some people do. That idea was too much, too... disturbing.

Jonce's procession was approximately four and a half to five miles long. An insane number of people came to the graveside. It was overwhelming to say the least. The funeral service was beautiful; my daddy did the graveside sermon and Jonce's best friend, Donny Parmer presented me with the flag from his casket (picture in book). The fact that they did these acts for Jonce's family and me are acts of love that defy human description.

Once the funeral was over, I saw people who had come just for the funeral from different states and made it just in time to the graveside. Afterwards, they greeted me, hugged me, and turned right around to travel home for meetings or other obligations. The fact that people did this just to try to ease my suffering and show their respect floors me even now. I know there are many people that were amazing and comforting to me during this time. I also know I left out many acts of kindness performed by these friends. I am sorry if I left anyone out.

I will say that there are close friends who were my foundation during and after this tragic experience and were there for me day and night. These amazing people cuddled me to sleep, fed me, ran errands, and listened to me endlessly. For those friends such as Cass, Jeff, Bart, Tina, Mark, Angela, Shonda, Haley, Donny, Tammie, Jimmy, Angela, Kelsey, Ali, Christie, and countless others, my gratitude and love are unending. The support the family and I received after the funeral was simply amazing. People filed in and out for weeks on end. It was extremely comforting and consoling for my soul.

Eventually though, the stream of condolence callers wanes off. People have lives, jobs, children, their own obligations. So here I was. It was done. Done. Funeral over. Jonce buried. Me, a widow with a teenage daughter. A new chapter. I can't recall a time in my life I ever felt more terrified or more lost.

10

*B*LESS IT. I THOUGHT *I* WAS

IN CONTROL…

"I have so many things to work on, and so many ways that I fail. But that's what grace is all about, and I constantly wake up every morning trying to get better, trying to improve, trying to walk closer to God."---Tim Tebow

I started writing this second part of the book on 7/22/2012, exactly two years after Jonce passed away. What strikes me most is the metamorphosis that I continue to experience. As the old saying goes, "change is the only constant in life." Overall, I can say that I am resistant to change, but sometimes, when change is forced upon you, the process can be a little easier.

During the second part of the book, I will skip over many specific things that happened, and get to the meat of this. First, let's start with overall changes during the past two years of my life. Over the last two years, I have struggled with the grief process, his family, school, legal issues, *multiple* funerals, my job, a move to a new house, a new relationship, and a few other odds and ends. Each change brought to light a new part of who I am that I didn't know.

I went through every stage of the grief cycle. A few times. I constantly asked "why?" I begged for forgiveness for falling short as a wife, not going to church, not forcing Jonce to go to church, not being a better parent to the kids, a better wife, being too self-involved, and numerous other things. More than once I cycled through the bargaining stage, with the thought being "If I ask for forgiveness and He gives it to me, maybe He will miraculously return Jonce." Obviously, that did not happen.

I find now that I am more vocal about my faith and my belief system. I am more understanding of others (most of the time), and I have found a new joy in serving others (*Philippians 2:1-4*). God enabled changes I never would have foreseen in my life, and He continues to bless me in ways that baffle me. When I completely allowed myself to open up to Him and let His plan for me just happen, I felt happier and freer than I had in a long time. All this time I thought I was in control. HA! Yeah, I wasn't, and I'm not now---and bless it---neither are you.

Immediately after Jonce's death, I began the administrative tasks that accompany being the administrator of an estate. The process actually helped to further solidify reality. Initially, the legal aspects and the process of cancelling mail, removing his name from our finances and personal property was a nightmare. More than once, I felt as if Muhammad Ali had pummeled me for ten solid rounds. Often, I felt like my insides were being twisted out and run over with a lawn mower. However, I think having to put on my "business hat" helped me adjust better. I gave many of Jonce's personal items to family and friends, and I nested in the house. I rearranged, changed some things, and left other things the same. If it was too painful, I put it away, if it was comforting, I let it keep its place.

Right after his death, in the days between his actual passing and the funeral, I had been bombarded with people stating I should hire a lawyer. Additionally, I got unsolicited calls from attorneys all over the state. I eventually decided that while what had happened was an accident, someone still needed to be held accountable. The children needed to be taken care of and I wanted to make sure that this type of senseless accident didn't happen again. I was then put in touch with a local attorney who was well regarded in this area.

Immediately upon meeting my attorney, P.J., I felt an immense amount of comfort. P.J. reminded me a little of my father. P.J. has a compassionate and gentle spirit that most attorneys lack. I knew that he had been placed in my path to really help me, not just get his percentage. Through my entire grieving process over the next year and a half, P.J. handled the Wrongful Death suit meticulously and with great care and compassion. After approximately a year and a half, a settlement was reached. I never once worried through that ordeal. I knew it was handled. God used P.J. to take care of things for us.

As far as the children were concerned these past two years, Becky lived with me, Michael and Brad lived on their own, and Daniel lived with his grandparents. Between the times of Jonce's death until roughly November of 2010, I fought for custody of Becky and won. Becky continued to live with me until August of 2011. At this point, she had decided she no longer wanted to live with me, so she moved to her grandparent's home with her brother Daniel. This actually floored me a little because I thought we had been getting along so much better, but apparently, she was feeling things she was not telling me. We had tried counseling for her, and I went to counseling myself. I encouraged her to go to counseling with me, but she did not want any part of it; she just wanted to leave.

Ultimately, I decided that this would probably be best for her at this point in her life. I had great guilt over this, as if I had let Jonce down in some way, but in the end, I can only do what I can do. Becky was determined to not like me or live with me, so I decided that some things just needed to be handled by God. Trying to force her to stay would have only ended in disaster, so I let go. She still lives with her grandparents and occasionally we communicate. She seems happy, which is all I ever wanted for her in the first place. Brad calls occasionally, and I rarely have had occasion to see or speak with Michael and Daniel.

I still talk to Jonce's mom and dad, as well as Jason and B.J. I also see and talk to his Aunt Peggy and Uncle Harvey, as well as some of his close cousins. I rarely speak to Jonce's stepbrothers, Joey and Shane. I have been told that divorce is similar to a death in some ways. When you divorce someone (I assume) that the family you had married into falls away naturally. The same thing occurs with a death. Eventually the widow or other members of the family find it awkward to communicate. I get that, and I love the family still, but everyone's life moves in different directions.

In addition, in the month after Jonce passed, I took a leave of absence from both work and school. In totality, I think I missed a month of each. The support from my Department of Human Resources (DHR) family and my school mentor were beyond description. The compassion and love of the men and women I worked with at DHR astounded me. It still does. Having the loyal friendships that I developed working there continues today, even though I am no longer employed there. Christie, my boss, lost her son in a tragic car accident not long after Jonce passed away. I can't begin to fathom the pain of losing a child. Somehow, though, through our losses, she and I became close. Her foundation of faith is awe-inspiring even if she doesn't think so.

Alison Sloan (Barry's wife, Jonce's fallen co-worker) was at DHR in another county, but was eventually brought to work where I was working. If she hadn't been able to move there, I am not sure how either of us would have fared. We have a sisterhood now, one forged by the blood of our husbands. Nothing will break it. Ever. Having her at work with me day-to-day was such a blessing and support, and I think she would say the same.

School completion was delayed after Jonce's death. I briefly thought about quitting, but that was a transient thought at best. I have worked too hard, and Jonce was so proud of me getting my PhD, that I didn't seriously consider quitting for longer than five minutes at a time. My mentor, Dr. Ayers, is an amazing man; he is supportive and encouraging. If it hadn't been for his guidance, I could have really destroyed my educational path. His support kept me on my path. Due in large part to Dr. Ayers's dedication to me, I was able to complete my requirements and graduated upon the final editing of this book.

The worst of the ongoing changes since his death is the sheer number of other people who have died. I quit counting at twelve or so. Friends, friends of friends, co-workers in the community I had worked with in the past, relatives of my fiancé (yes, fiancé), and the list goes on. I think that after the death of a spouse, one gleans a more comprehensive understanding of death. Yes, I have lost a parent, but you expect that in life. Your parents go first, right? In the great circle of life, the parent goes first. However, losing a spouse is just different. When the person you are supposed to "grow old with" dies, it leaves an unfathomable echoing void.

After the death of a spouse, when someone you know loses someone too soon or in an unexpected manner (someone's child, a suicide, a friend, a young acquaintance, someone suffering from a disease, etc...), it's almost as if you can feel their pain more intensely. This is especially so when you encounter another widow or widower.

The saying, "I know exactly how you feel," is never more true. You *do* know, and you'd take it for them if you could. It's not a club I want any woman or man to join. If I estimated, I would say I know of and attended viewings and/or funerals for probably three of four people who have lost their spouse since I lost Jonce. I know I will attend more, because people die, and that is the way this world works. Every loss is going to be painful and depressing every single time; there's no way around that either.

Every loss can devastate you, and each one of these funerals will suck your soul if you let it. I *choose* not to. I don't know *why* Jonce was not able to remain with us, and I am not going to know why - not until *He* chooses to let me know. Last time I checked, God doesn't check with me on His decisions, and I don't imagine He will start asking my opinion on matters any time soon. All I can do is offer is the same love and support that has been shown to me. God provides those of us left behind an extraordinary amount of grace and peace if we are open to receive it.

Of the many changes in my life since Jonce's death, the two most joyous have been the move to a different house and my marriage. Yes, I said marriage. The new house is a little outside Guntersville, Alabama. The house is quiet and spacious, I have wild turkey and deer in my back yard, and an almost tame and adorable raccoon (affectionately referred to as Rocky or Bandit). The backyard is covered in trees and large limestone rocks, it is peaceful, and it is away from whatever drama may ensue elsewhere. I like my "drama-free happy bubble." I looked at several houses to rent, all of which were rented out from underneath me, or put on the market to sell rather than rent. But this one was the one that God picked. Nothing fell through, everything has gone smoothly, and the home is perfect, perfect to make a new home for the next chapter of my life. The house Jonce and I shared is rented by a sweet couple with a large family. The husband in that family is also a rabid Alabama Football fan. The result seems very... divine. I became emotional when I moved out, but it's just a house. I still have all the wonderful memories I have of Jonce.

On 7/28/2012, I started my new chapter. Did I ever think I would marry again? Oh Goodness. Uhhhh, NO. Immediately after Jonce's passing, I was determined I would be a widow all the days of my life. I would mourn, wail, and never be married again. I would not entertain even the slightest possibility that I would have to endure that kind of loss again. Then I had periods where the idea that I might marry again crept inside my mind. Eventually I knew I would remarry, and shockingly, I *wanted* to remarry. I am tenderhearted and have a great capacity to love. I love being married, and I love "belonging" to someone. Being married is the most wonderful feeling in the world. I loved being married to Jonce. I loved having that one person in my life that I could be with, confide in, and count on, and vice versa. I consider my remarrying a testament to Jonce. I loved being married to Jonce so much that I wanted to marry again.

Is it possible I will experience that loss again? Will my new husband pass this world before I do? Will I have to endure this kind of pain again? Possibly. However, I realized, if I hadn't married Jonce, and thereby hadn't endured losing him, I also would have missed out on the most precious relationship I had had in my life up to that point. So, given my choices, I could live alone with my cats, close myself off, and never have another meaningful personal relationship again, *or* I could open myself up again, regardless of what the future holds. I opted for the latter, and it is the best choice I could have ever made.

The hysterical thing is, as I look back, I also understand that *I had absolutely no hand in the fact I would remarry.* That wasn't *my* plan. That was *His* plan. God is the one who brought this to me. He is the one who placed my new husband in my path. He is the one who put on my heart that He made me to love (*1 John 4:7-8; 19 NIV*). God didn't want me to live alone. God didn't want me miserable all the rest of the days of my life (*Genesis 2:18 NIV*).

My new husband was actually a friend of Jonce's. They grew up in the same area, hung out with one another, and were good friends. They lost touch for a period because life and other obligations got in the way. However, in 2007, Jonce and Ronny had reconnected. From 2007-2010, Ronny and his oldest daughter, Haley, would come over to the house to watch football games, watch NASCAR races, and attend birthdays and special events with us.

After Jonce died, I had serious "faith issues" and general questions about the "hereafter." I wondered what things meant scripturally and spiritually about marriage after a death, about heaven, souls, and other general questions. Ronny was the one who helped me sort those issues out, he was the one who let me call him at two in the morning and ask stupid questions and cry just to cry. I had other friends who supported me in this way, but Ronny was the one whom

I felt the most comfortable having these sorts of conversations. He was the one person that I could be around and *just breathe*. I could comfortably ask any question, voice any worry, complain about any aspect of my life on any level, and there was no apprehension. I didn't have to have a discussion or ask a question and simultaneously wonder if something I said came out wrong. Ronny never once conveyed judgment, doubt, or scorn about the way I felt or what I expressed. His eyes held only understanding and comfort. Amazing isn't it? In a time like this, I couldn't articulate what I needed from people, I felt like I couldn't make anyone understand how bad I was hurting, and then God provided me Ronny. That my friend is called God's Providence.

God's Providence is the most amazing thing really. I mentioned earlier that God actually prepared me for the death of my husband. Now that you have read a small summation of the changes in my life since his death, let's back up and I will show you two specific instances of His Grace and Providence. These are instances of His Grace and Providence that I hadn't been able to see clearly until some time had passed.

About a year and a half or so before his death, Jonce and I began riding motorcycles less and hanging out with new friends at the lake more. I referenced this group earlier as "The Boat Crew." We normally spent weekends hanging out with Jason and B.J. (my brother and sister-in-law), but life changes and new friends on both ends dwindled the amount of time we spent together. This new group of friends turned out to be my life raft after Jonce died.

It took me a while, but I realized one day that God had intervened to place these people in our lives on purpose. God provided these friends so that I had a solid foundation to comfort and console me after Jonce's passing. Not that Jason and B.J. weren't comforting or consoling, but after Jonce's death, they had their own grief and turmoil to contend with. I feel that God provided me a foundation to rest on during my intense grief without my having to burden his brother's family with my grief on top of their own.

Then there's Alison Sloan. My sister, my friend. As I stated earlier, Alison had been the intern at DHR when I worked there, and we built a co-worker friendship before she was hired in another county. Barry applied for a job with the company my husband worked for because Jonce, Alison, and I had urged him to apply. In retrospect, I am completely convinced that mine and Alison's friendship, and the arrangement of Barry's new job with Jonce's company had God's handiwork all over it.

"Providence" is God providing for you the things and people in your life that you need in any given season. You might not know it at the time, and often times, it is after some event that you realize He had protected and provided for you all along. This scripture from Exodus most vividly gives me a picture of not just God's providence, but God's protection as well [**emphasis mine**].

Exodus 33:18-23 NIV:
*"**18** Then Moses said, "I pray You, show me Your glory!" **19** And He said, "I Myself will make all My goodness pass before you, and will proclaim the name of the LORD before you; and I will be gracious to whom I will be gracious, and will show compassion on whom I will show compassion." [**Providence**] **20** But He said, "You cannot see My face, for no man can see Me and live!" **21** Then the LORD said, "Behold, there is a place by Me, and you shall stand there on the rock ; **22** and it will come about, while My glory is passing by, that I will put you in the cleft of the rock and cover you with My hand until I have passed by [**protection**]. **23** "Then I will take My hand away and you shall see My back, but My face shall not be seen."*

I first heard this scripture referenced in bible study by my friend Lena. It makes me weepy when I read it now. Through this verse, I see the time leading up to and the day of Jonce's death. For a year and a half preceding his death, it was as if God had put me in a place to provide some protection of what was to come. He placed me in the "cleft of the rock" known as my circle of friends. Once the storm of Jonce's death was upon me, He covered me with his hand to protect me. I still hurt, mourned, and grieved (and still do) the loss of my husband, but His hand was over me the entire time (verse 22). He protected me from tools the enemy may have used against me. He protected me from an onslaught of depression, anxiety, ill will towards the driver of the truck, and hateful spirit of heart (verse 22). After the storm had settled, I realized He was in front of me, walking forward, His back to me, His hand extended behind Him beckoning me to grab a hold of Him (verse 23).

11

*L*ORD,

PLACE YOUR ARM AROUND ME
AND POSSIBLY YOUR HAND OVER
MY MOUTH. AMEN.

I didn't aimlessly wander through the last two years emotionally unscathed. Getting to this place was an emotional roller coaster. Any widow or widower will understand what I mean when I say, everyone, and I mean, *"everyone has an opinion."* There is a "social expectancy" that widows and widowers contemplate and often times fear. There are things that a widow or widower has to contend with that other losses don't bring.

Still, I have to ask God to keep His arm around me but to cover my mouth if it looks like He needs to. What's contained in this chapter are my emotional struggles from Jonce's death until now. When I say emotional struggles, I mean the ones that originate from how I perceived myself versus how I felt others perceived me. It's not all bad mind you, but let's just say that *before* reconnecting and strengthening my relationship with God, I had moments where I wanted to tear people asunder. Literally.

Everyone's mourning and grief processes are different, but I do believe that widows and widowers ride a similar undercurrent of change. Our experiences as a collective group are more similar than not. As a reader, you may see areas that are or were similar to areas you contended with, some different. In the end, while change is a pain in the rear end most of the time, I feel I am continuing to grow into a much better person. I am more faithful, more merciful, and gracious with others, and, most excitingly for me, a new creation in God. I am not the only one who has noticed this change. I have had several people inside and outside of my church family tell me that they see positive changes in me (*2 Corinthians 5:17; 2 Corinthians 3:18*). That alone tells me I am doing something right. I know I am changed because I am not the "same me" I used to be. Thank God.

My Perception/Myth: The [perceived] wallowing period of a widow or a widower is directionally proportional to how much that widow or widower loved their deceased spouse.

When your spouse dies, the world, for a little while, comes to a grinding halt. It's akin to driving eighty miles an hour and slamming into a brick wall with your car staying intact. That is to say that the car stops whole, but the inertia of that high speed propels the person inside the car (you), through the windshield, and into the brick wall head on, never slowing down. You're a mangled mess, but no other cars around you wrecked. People drive around the wreckage, shake their heads, and say a prayer of thanks that it wasn't them. Life moves on. People still work, bills still come due, kids still have basic living needs that need to be met, and you still need to eat, clean, and carry on.

Some people don't carry on, or they feel like they can't. Some people wallow, drift into a deep depression, and neglect themselves physically, emotionally, and mentally. Some widows/widowers can't function enough to take care of themselves, let alone children.

Others, mourn and grieve, and sooner rather than later, pick up, go back to work, take care of things, and maybe seek counseling. There are also those in between these two places, and still others that cycle back and forth repeatedly. All of these responses are very natural and expected. Different people handle things differently. It's part of what makes us unique, what makes us human. The truth really comes down to this: *You never truly understand something until it happens to you.*

I knew that people handle grief differently. I knew all these responses were natural, but I only had one response for a long time - guilt. Complete and utter misplaced guilt. No one who really loves me or knows me ever thought... for a second... that I did not love my husband. No one who loves me and knows me ever thought that because I picked up and "got back to it" meant that I wasn't grieving or that I was trying to forget my husband. On the contrary, most of the people I know repeatedly told me how "strong" I was or that I "inspired" them. If they only knew the number of private moments I had, I am sure that opinion might change. Be that as it may, God helped me let go of that guilt. I could get on with life. I had things to do, a kid to try to raise, a job, a lawsuit to deal with, school to finish, papers to write, and eventually a book to start.

My Perception/Myth: Hanging out with a male friend after the death of one's husband means you are "dating..." Gheesh.

From my early experience after Jonce's death, I felt that the conventional wisdom (at least in a small town) says that the widow or the widower is supposed to sit on their spouse's tombstone and ring out their hanky for the foreseeable future. That's not me. I went on, I went back to work after a month off, I worked like a dog, I went out a couple of times with friends (male and female both), and I threw myself into things to get myself moving again. I had to, I don't wallow, and it's not how I am wired. I also feel that my father and granddaddy's mourning processes also had a great influence on the way I handled social situations and eventually yes, dating.

Dad remarried nine months after my mom died. Granddaddy has lost two wives and has remarried both times within six months. The men in my family love to be married; they consider it an honor to be a husband. They feel God called them not to just be married, but to be *great* husbands. They do it very well. However, I also watched God's providence after my mom passed.

Daddy was just pitiful after mom died. Bless his heart, he blamed himself because mom had been sick and he had not realized it. She had been taking care of him because he had been sick. You can see where the guilt train ran over him in the grieving process. Then about three months after mom died, I walked through the kitchen when I was visiting and helping dad, and stopped. I whipped my head around, took in a nice deep breath, and cut my eyes.

"You have a date. I smell it. You're wearing Clubman. You have a *date*." I grinned. "Who is it?"

"The little redhead from church"

"Uh huh. Ok. Behave yourself."

That was that. No judgment from me. I had watched daddy for the last three months become a heap and a shell of who he was. I was supportive of him going on a little date. My *mother would have wanted him to as well.* The providence is this. Pam, the little redhead from church, had never met my mom, but she had such an overwhelming feeling of sadness when she had heard about mom's passing that she volunteered to keep the visitor's children in the nursery during mom's funeral. Pam did not know my mom or my dad. She only found out about daddy being the widower of that funeral right before their first date. Tell me God didn't have his hand on that and I will sell you ocean front property in the Midwest.

So, given the experiences of the men in my life, I didn't have an issue going out with friends or hanging out with male friends specifically after Jonce died. For crying out loud, the friends I was hanging out with were *our* friends. Now, you all remember I mentioned Ronny. This was one of those friends. For times immediately following Jonce's death, I hung out with Ronny a lot because his presence and support was comfortable and I felt like I could talk to him about anything.

We did eventually start dating. I know that was neither my intent nor his, when we first began spending time together. I think God had everything to do with it. I probably followed most closely to dad's pattern here. I think I have pinpointed comfortably that Ronny and I really started "dating" if you will, about three and a half to four months after Jonce died. Truth be known, I think I felt we were actually dating sooner (probably closer to three months), but the guilt kept me from admitting it to Ronny or myself.

I also heard shortly after Jonce's passing that I apparently "hooked up" with my friend's husband. Both my friends and I found that hysterical. My girlfriend was a little more upset about it, because she knew neither her husband nor I would ever do such a thing. However, she was also livid someone would even give it credence. Given the stellar woman that she is, she was angry not only for me, but that people would drum up a rumor like that and impugn her marriage.

Then there was a recent rumor a few months ago that I had been dating a chiropractor in town and we just broke up. LOL. Huh. News to me. I had been engaged to Ronny for four months by this point. Alison Sloan rightly put that misinformation to rest. I know other little rumors have passed around, but I don't really care. Once I realized that God had sent me this wonderful man, I really didn't give two rips anymore what people thought. When this sort of thing presents itself, a person has to maintain a sense of humor. If you can't, depression and anger will drag you down. Marriage is until "Death Do You Part." I wasn't going to allow anyone make me feel ashamed, upset, or indignant. I decided that if God had decided to place someone in my life after Jonce died, then so be it.

I am a new creature in Christ, but lest we forget, I am still human. Although saved, I still become crabby when I have reached my limits. On more than one occasion, I could see a little condemnation in the eyes of someone when they realized I was dating someone. I have always been polite (mostly) about it. I did have choice words for a person or two regarding this subject but luckily, the Holy Spirit reined me back in before I got nasty about it. The truth is that, the people who really love me never thought I didn't love Jonce, or even that I wasn't still grieving when I started dating Ronny. Most people who knew we were dating were happy that I found someone who was sweet to me and seemed to bring me some happiness after what I had endured. My point is this: I know my heart, I know Ronny's heart, and I know *My God*. I know what He has given me, and I know how magnificent Ronny and his girls are to me. At one point, I never thought I would have a family again. I just count myself immeasurably blessed that God saw fit to bring us together, no matter how tragic the circumstances were that started our journey.

Grieving

We are promised that when we die, that being absent from the body is to be present with God (*2 Corinthians 5:6*). Grief has its time and purpose (*Ecclesiastes 3:1-4*), but if the loss takes up residence in one's spirit instead of this promise, it can become a tool of the enemy. Some people will meditate on the loss until the tools of the enemy become many (anger, blame, slander, hopelessness, separation, etc....). The bible records grieving periods lasting from seven days to seventy days (*Deuteronomy 34:8; Genesis 50:10 and 23*). Some people may grieve for a longer period, but we should not *worship* the person we grieve. We were meant to grieve and mourn for a time and then to rejoice that they were born into eternal life (*Romans 12:15; Psalm 30:11-12*). Christ also promised to take our heartache and grief and turn it into joy.

Jeremiah 31:13: I will turn their mourning into gladness; I will give them comfort and joy instead of sorrow

Psalm 30:5: For his anger lasts only a moment, but his favor lasts a lifetime; weeping may stay for the night, but rejoicing comes in the morning.

My Perception/Myth: There are certain things you do because they are EXPECTED of you to do; they are a testament to how much you loved your spouse.

Yeah, I know, boneheaded thought pattern, but that's where my brain was. I mean, where else would it be after Jonce died? For instance, let's take Becky and my dating Ronny, and move into what the real problem *really* was (again, my opinion). I am sure there are people who thought, "What is she thinking? She has Becky to think about! Is she trying to replace Jonce with Ronny for Becky?!!!" My response... Uh. NO.

I thought that since Ronny had primary custody of his children and was a good friend with Jonce, that his youngest child, Lauren, would enjoy hanging around Becky. I also thought because Ronny had lost his father at age six, Becky might be able to talk to him about stuff that I could not (I lost my mom at twenty-eight not fourteen). Ronny and both of his girls were and always have been a tremendously good influence on Becky, I asked her how she felt about Ronny and I dating, and she said she was fine with it, and she wanted me to be happy. She stated she loved Lauren and Haley and she liked Ronny and thought he was sweet.

In retrospect, I should have probably been a little more intuitive where that was concerned, but I was taking Becky at her word. After she moved out and some time has passed, I do believe that she did take issue with my dating, but wasn't being honest with me about the situation at the time. I think our falling out a year after Jonce's death was because of several things. Mainly, I felt like, at that point, she really just didn't like me, and that she felt she would have been better off if I had died instead of her father. I also think she was resentful of my having a male friend and that somehow, I was trying to replace her father.

I really believe that it wouldn't have mattered what I did, she was going to be mad at everything because her father had been taken from her. I know Becky never wanted to live with me. I found out later, through a friend, that Becky had stated that she hadn't wanted to live with me right after Jonce died. Apparently, she had just said she did because other influential adults in her life were telling her it was the best thing for her to do.

I fought for custody of Becky for two reasons. One, she said she wanted me to, and I wanted her to stay with me. Secondly, I thought it was what people *expected* of me as Jonce's wife. The first reason is a good reason, the latter... not so much. I will again practice honesty with modesty here. Suffice it to say, I think she felt that I wasn't her "family," and she wanted to be with her father's family. I understand that completely. I was hurt when she moved out, but she is a *child*. Harboring resentment or anger towards a child in pain is just wrong and absurd. I won't do it.

I understood, even if she didn't, that her choice of words and actions were driven by the loss of her father. I also understand that my choices probably did influence the situation, but I don't believe I made any choices that were damaging to her. Truth be known, I think

I tried harder as a parent after Jonce died. I started back to church because I realized the many ways I had fallen short the years prior to Jonce's death. I was more patient, I was fairer, I didn't let my temper get to me the way it had before, and I just was calmer and more even.

I spent more time with her (or tried to) on an individual basis, and yes, I included her in outings with Ronny and his kids. In retrospect, I feel that may have seemed a little "pushy" to Becky, and I should have noticed that. I was probably a bit too caught up in trying to get life back to a new normal for her, and it may have come across as if I was forcing something on her when that *was not* my intent.

Individual counseling was ineffective with her, she refused family counseling with me, and meetings with our youth pastor were ineffective. All she wanted to do was leave, because, according to her in the summer of 2011, I wasn't her "family." Ouch. After a battle of wills and stalling, I let her live with her grandparents, and they obtained final legal custody in the summer 2012. I think it is better for our relationship with the current arrangement in some ways. She was texting me (and I still have the texts) that she is remorseful for the stuff she said, that she knows her dad would want me to be happy, and that she is happy for me. She has even said she occasionally regretted moving out.

Becky is a child who has endured a lot in her young life, and I do realize this. I do also realize that I should have never obtained her custody out a misperception of what I thought was expected of me by everyone else. Not a smart move, but a lesson learned that is not to be repeated. I love Becky, I think she has the potential to be a great young woman, and I have told her this. I also told her that she could contact me whenever she needs to, if she needs me. For now, that's the way it remains.

I choose to have faith and believe wholeheartedly that this is an instance of God's providence that hasn't produced any fruit yet. I think God is at work in her, and I *know* He's at work in me. I pray that in the future, Becky will learn more of what it means to be a woman of her word, a woman of stellar reputation, and a woman who fears God. I pray that for me, He continues to mold me into what He would have me be, a better mother than I had been in the past, a woman who continues to fear God and grow in His Word, and a woman who lives by faith, and not by sight. I also pray daily to be a woman of grace and love, *not a woman defined by* fear, shame, or my own stupid human shortcomings.

12

ABOUNDING GRACE, MERCY, FORGIVENESS, FAITH, PEACE...

Bible study author, Beth Moore is simply amazing. I have found that her teachings speak to me tremendously. I have almost completed the study on James, and Ronny and I are about to start another one called "A Heart Like His." I also find myself you-tubing videos of her some mornings for a daily gem. I recently watched her teach on getting out of "the pit" that we so often find ourselves in. Whether we are thrown in by someone/something else's doing, we slip in, or jump in by willful commission of sin, we can get out. Either we credit God getting us out, or we credit another human being in doing so. By believing another person pulled us from whatever pit we find ourselves, and then acting as though that person is our savior, we lend ourselves over to bondage. I hadn't really thought of it that way before, but it made sense to me.

I was, with the death of my husband, thrown into a pit. A dark, nasty pit, where I could easily have given into depression, sadness, and complete despair. I grieved (and still do), but allowing the pit to become "home" was not an option. I think I might still be clawing my way up the side of that pit if I hadn't been blessed with my church family. I credit my friends with *helping* me out of the pit. However, God's and His abounding grace pulled me free. He graciously used my friends and their unending love to lift me a little higher to the edge of the pit so that I could peek out to see what lay beyond.

I was resistant in going back to church. Jonce and I had not gone together because Jonce felt because he drank and smoked, and occasionally used colorful language, that it was hypocritical for him to go to church. We had a couple of conversations about this; and more than once he and I both expressed an urge to return to church, but we never seemed able to take that step. Anger at God wasn't really what had kept me away. It was some stupid notion that I would be secretly judged or criticized by others for coming to church when I hadn't been coming before Jonce's death. I feared what my friends might think, and I feared what these churchgoers might believe about me.

"Awwww, look, she's decided to come to church. It's just so sad that it took her spouse dying to bring her in the door. So sad. Bless her heart. I wonder how long she'll continue to come?"

This reaction couldn't have been further from my personal experience.

Becky begged me to go to service with her. I reluctantly gave in the first week in February 2011. I took her to the early service at 9:30, and promptly heard complaints for the next twenty minutes on the ride home---

"Gggahhhh! NO ONE goes to early service, we have to go to the 10:30 service, and 9:30 is soooo boring!"

Yang yang yang…. Blah blah blah….

"Uuhhh! Fine, we will go to the late service next week, gees, happy now?"

I took Ronny with me because he had been to this particular church before, and I needed an anchor. My anxiety was high and I needed another adult to hold my hand. It doesn't sound like it, but I really am a big girl. Here. I will prove it. I can admit when I am wrong. *I was totally, completely, and utterly* **wrong**. First, Becky was right. More of my contemporaries go to the 10:30 service, and I was much more comfortable in the later service. Secondly, even though the fears were there, I never once felt out of place. I was welcomed and wrapped in love the minute I hit the door. The later service did have more people I recognized, even several of the women I worked with.

There is that providence thing again; it sneaks and wraps you up, warm fuzzies and all.

Third, my presence did not test the structural integrity of the church building. No rafters came down, the earth did not swallow me whole, and Jesus, himself, did not descend into the sanctuary and point a damning finger at me, asking me why I had defiled His temple with my existence. This might be an overstatement. I never really expected these things, but when you have wandered away for so long and Satan has shaken your faith, it can feel like impending doom awaits you in the vestibule.

For the last thirteen years, I drank, cussed, smoked (yes, I still smoke, I am a work in progress), and I had not been the best parental figure. I had a tendency to be selfish and I hadn't pushed the issue of coming to church with Jonce when he was alive. Overall, I had been running the other direction so hard, so fast, for so long that I was scared to go back, scared I would be mocked, ridiculed, and considered unworthy.

Over the course of several months, I found myself thoroughly enjoying myself on Sunday and even a little testy when I couldn't go to church for one reason or another. I must say though, the first month was confusing for me. I had refused to go to church for so long, that I was befuddled when I would cry in church during the musical worship portion of the service. The sermons were great, but I why was I turning into a blithering idiot during worship music? Two words people… Holy *Spirit*.

Musical worship portions of services used to annoy me as a teenager because they seemed so long. At fourteen, I wanted to get to it, get it done, and go eat lunch. Now, I want the worship portion of the service to last longer. I never have been a big music person. I like it well enough, but I don't identify with music on a personal level very often, or at least I didn't use to. Music helps us in our spiritual warfare (*2 Chronicles 20:21-22*). Now, I listen to worship music all the time---in the car, in the house, sing it to myself---and become a crying, sobbing mess more often than not. Some people blow their car windows out with Metallica, I blow mine with the Christian worship band "Building 429." I find that worship music speaks to my soul. It helps me express emotions, fears, concerns, joys, and triumphs that I can't verbalize with my own inadequate words. I believe that God knows that's what "gets me," what makes me think, and opens me to feel His presence. He uses what you will allow Him to use.

I tend to think in imagery where My Father is concerned, and I will use it quite a bit. I liken God to an earthly fatherly figure (like my dad). Thus, when I picture Him, I picture Him interacting with me as my dad would. Often He is exasperated but loving, and yes, knowing more than I do. Imagine that. So, when I was peering over the edge of the pit that could have swallowed me, what did I see? I literally picture God smiling, maybe even chuckling a little bit, sitting on the porch in a chair, and as I walk up, we have this conversation:

"No, offense sweetie, but you look a little rough."

"Well, it's no wonder, you just left me hanging like that, what did you expect?"

"I never left you. I've called for you this whole time."

"*No. No, you did not!* I would have heard you! Have you heard your call? It's kinda hard to miss."

"I am not hard to miss, but when you run around plugging your ears with your fingers and yelling 'la-la-la-la-la-la!' how well do you expect to hear me?"

Busted. All of the imagery to say this; When I peered over the edge and crawled out, what I saw was a path home paved in grace, mercy, forgiveness, peace, faith, and a loving God with a sense of humor and unending patience.

"Then you will call upon Me and go and pray to Me, and I will listen to you. And you will seek Me and find Me. When your search for me with all your heart"

--- Jeremiah 29:12-13
NIV

Grace
Ephesians 2:4-9: *"But God, being rich in mercy, because of the great love with which He loved us, even when we were dead in our trespasses, made us alive together with Christ— by grace you have been saved—and raised us up with Him and seated us with Him in the heavenly places in Christ Jesus, so that in the coming ages He might show the immeasurable riches of His grace in kindness toward us in Christ Jesus. For by grace you have been saved through faith. And this is not your own doing; it is the gift of God, not a result of works, so that no one may boast."*

For me, this captures the definition of grace in scripture. Grace is unmerited favor or getting something you don't deserve. I certainly had not been worthy or deserving ever; nor am I still worthy of it. However, He gives it to me. Every day. *I am His child.* Ronny made a fabulous allusion to this concept in imagery for me one day, and it just nailed it. He compared the concept to the mangy dog. I will paraphrase:

> "I picture kind of like this. Let's say there is some mangy dog that is nasty, sick, matted, smelly, a dog on its last leg. I might be inclined to put the poor thing out of its misery. But then my daughter comes up and drapes herself on that dog, and says "No daddy! You can't!!! I love him!---he's *mine!*' That's what I mean. We are all mangy, sick, nasty, matted creatures. In some people's opinion, we might be better off to be put out of our misery, but Jesus intervened, draped Himself on us, and said, "No Daddy, I love them, these are *mine.*"

We don't deserve Grace, we haven't earned it, we never will, yet, Jesus stood in our place and took it on Himself so that we might have it through faith in Him. Aren't you glad God loves His son so much that He refuses to pull the trigger on you? I am eternally grateful.

Mercy

In short, mercy is the inverse of grace; not getting what you do deserve or having punishment withheld. In clicking, flipping, and scrolling through scriptures on mercy, I found Job 33:27-30 (NIV), particularly poignant, given the "pit" reference from earlier:

Job 33:27-30: *"I sinned and perverted what was right, but I did not get what I deserved. He redeemed my soul from going down to the pit [**or pulled me from the pit, my emphasis**], and I will live to enjoy the light of life." God does all these things to a man--twice, even three times--to turn back his soul from the pit, that the light of life may shine on him."*

Like grace, I know I am not, nor will ever be worthy of His mercy. God gives both His grace and mercy freely, vastly, limitlessly. Mercy does not end in repenting your sins and accepting His salvation by grace or in wrath and eternal punishment. It begins when you put your faith in Him. I will not go all fire and brimstone on you, because, well frankly, I am not well versed enough, and I too am not partial to someone scaring me into something as precious as my salvation.

I will tell you that, for me personally, after Jonce died, God called me out. I took stock of where I had been, what I had been doing, what I had not been doing, what I really truly wanted, and what I really wanted to change. For a long time after Jonce died, I took stock, but I had no answers. I wasn't sure what I wanted. However, I did know several things.

- I wanted to be happy.
- I didn't want to be sad anymore.
- I didn't want to feel guilty for things that happened or didn't happen.
- I wanted unabashed forgiveness for the way I had wandered.
- I didn't want to feel miserable for things I couldn't change.
- I didn't want to feel accountable or beholden to anyone out of a. feeling of obligation.
- I wanted to be a better person.
- I wanted to feel something more/bigger than me.
- I did NOT want to go through this again if I could help it.
- I wanted to feel comforted and unconditionally loved again.

I grew up in church and I knew better than to believe God would ever abandon me. I knew I wanted a relationship with God, but I had been so far displaced from that relationship with God, that I didn't recognize how to come back to Him. What I wanted was to go home, to come back to God. I didn't realize that until I found a church family where I felt really loved and comfortable. God knew what I needed, and again, provided it for me, readily and with a glad and loving heart. However, a little something goes with that - *accountability*. That, to me, was the scary part of all of this. Yes, I got everything on that list except maybe the next to last. I might have to endure losing a spouse again, but I wouldn't miss having the spouse for anything in this world. Being married is one of those amazing things that make this world bearable.

In recent years I made sure I was "unavailable for accountability." Part of the truth I had to face about myself was that if I had been doing right and attending church, or even able to get Jonce to go with me, we would have been accountable for the things we learned. So, what I mean when I say God "called me out," is that I got a little tap on the shoulder and a message from on High. The one-sided conversation went a little something like this:

> Sweetheart, yes, you can have all those things you wanted. I want to give them to you badly, and I will give them freely to you. But you do realize, that once you start to learn my Word, you learn what is expected of you, there is no shirking the responsibility, I expect you to be obedient.

So, yes, while it is scary, it is completely doable. I have wandered and gotten lost, been rebellious, testy, downright hateful, and rebuked God (on more than one occasion). If He's willing to show me grace and mercy, and He just wants me to be obedient, it's not asking that much is it? For me, no, it's not. I am not saying God lets me get away with everything and then I just repent and move on down the road. Occasionally, I have believed that His mercy was hidden or withheld, to teach me a lesson, to discipline me, or to rebuke me for something I knew better to do in the first place. What I have come to learn is that this is NOT true. God's mercy is *always* present; we just do not always recognize it until the time of hardship has passed. I find that these times when I felt that His Mercy was withheld, were often the times that I have stepped outside of His authority over my life.

I thank God that He never withholds His mercy from me, considering some of the stuff I have pulled in my day; I wouldn't blame Him if He had. In my opinion, I think guardian angles do not get near the credit they deserve. I think the Lord's angels work at breakneck speed dispensing His mercy on our sorry selves. Ronny joked once that when he gets to heaven anyone will be able to easily spot his guardian angels. They will be the ones with "smoking wings, laying prostrate, & praising God" that Ronny arrived, so they could take a breather.

I have also learned that if He gives me mercy, I should also show mercy to others. He expects it of me. It is easier said than done sometimes, but completely worth the effort. For instance, I could have refused to show the driver of the truck that backed into Jonce's tower mercy, and I could have been a real idiot and refused to forgive him. I could have done things to make the man's life a living hell on earth. To what end? I just learned the parable of the unmerciful servant, and I think it describes the concept of being merciful to others better than I ever could.

Matthew 18:23-35 (NIV):

"Therefore, the kingdom of heaven is like a king who wanted to settle accounts with his servants. As he began the settlement, a man who owed him ten thousand talents was brought to him. Since he was not able to pay, the master ordered that he and his wife and his children and all that he had be sold to repay the debt. The servant fell on his knees before him. 'Be patient with me,' he begged, 'and I will pay back everything.' The servant's master took pity on him, canceled the debt and let him go. But when that servant went out, he found one of his fellow servants who owed him a hundred denarii. He grabbed him and began to choke him. 'Pay back what you owe me!' he demanded. His fellow servant fell to his knees and begged him, 'Be patient with me, and I will pay you back.' But he refused. Instead, he went off and had the man thrown into prison until he could pay the debt. When the other servants saw what happened, they were greatly distressed and went and told their master everything that had happened. Then the master called the servant in. 'You wicked servant,' he said, 'I canceled all that debt of yours because you begged me to. Shouldn't you have had mercy on your fellow servant just as I had on you?' In anger his master turned him over to the jailers to be tortured, until he should pay back all he owed. This is how my heavenly Father will treat each of you unless you forgive your brother from the heart."

Forgiveness

Countless Scriptures address forgiveness, and I couldn't possible list them all. I have never been one to hold a grudge (when I was younger, maybe, but not any longer). More often than not, I hate being mad at someone and I hate someone being mad at me (drives me completely nuts). In perusing the Scriptures though, several verses in particular stand out to me because of *my* attitude towards forgiveness regarding Jonce's death.

Luke 6:38 (NIV) – "Give, and it will be given to you. A good measure, pressed down, shaken together and running over, will be poured into your lap. For with the measure you use, it will be measured to you."

2 Corinthians 2:5-8 (NIV) – "Now if anyone has caused pain, he has caused it not to me, but in some measure—not to put it too severely—to all of you. For such a one, this punishment by the majority is enough, so you should rather turn to forgive and comfort him, or he may be overwhelmed by excessive sorrow. So I beg you to reaffirm your love for him."

Ephesians 4:31-32 (NIV) – "Let all bitterness and wrath and anger and clamor and slander be put away from you, along with all malice. Be kind to one another, tenderhearted, forgiving one another, as God in Christ forgave you."

God gave his only child to atone for the sins of us lowly undeserving creatures so that we might be able to spend eternity with Him (*John 3:16*). I am floored if I really allow that to settle on my spirit. He sent His own child. He *knew* that He would be beaten, bruised, tortured, maimed, hung on a cross, spit on, and die a painful worldly death. He sat there and watched the entire thing unfold, yet God still forgave us at the beseeching of His only son. If I can't allow myself to forgive someone, it almost feels like I am slapping God in the face. Forgiveness is not easy, and it does hurt to give it to someone sometimes, but the peace that follows is extraordinary.

The driver of the thirty-three-foot bucket truck *did not* get up that morning and say, "You know what, I am going to use that truck at work today and kill someone." Of this, I am 1000% sure. I met the driver of the truck in the spring of 2012. He had been so tormented by what he had accidently done. He had been ripped apart, remorseful, and just pitiful. Being able to look me in the eye and apologize was all he had to give me. He couldn't give me back my husband or my life with him. To some people "I am so sorry" may not be enough. For me it was.

Truth be told, I forgave that man, almost immediately. I even asked Jonce's boss on the phone that day how the driver of the truck was doing. What good does it do me to condemn him, hate him, wish him dead, or wish ill on his life or that of his family? Each one of us, due to inattention, a stupid mistake, or a misunderstanding could be a hair's breath away from being the cause of something tragic. I forgave him, and all I could do was pray that he learned something from the accident, that he changed something about the way he worked, or trained other people.

When I told him that, he looked like I had hit him with a 2x4. Some people have told me, "I just couldn't forgive something like that," "I could never forgive someone like that." These people couldn't see being able to "let it go." What some people don't understand is this: My forgiveness to someone for a wrong is not just for that person's benefit, it's for mine as well. I refuse to live a life consumed by hate, heartache, and ill will toward another person. That is not why God put me here.

Beth Moore's bible study on James talks about living the "good life." Part of that life is being able to "yield" to others. Forgiving is the "biggest act of yielding that you will ever do" (Beth Moore, 2011). When she taught this, it spoke to me, and she explained it in a way I will not do it justice, but here goes. When you forgive someone it can feel like you are just "giving up" and the forgiveness you give just kind of just disappears into oblivion. The truth is that you are not "giving up" anything. By forgiving someone, you are "yielding up" something. You are "yielding" your pain, anguish, sadness, hurt, and anger over to God. There is a difference in "yielding" and "giving up."

When Jesus died on the cross, He didn't "give up" His spirit; He *committed it up* [yielded] unto His Father *(Matthew 27:50 ESV)*. Some versions of Scripture do use the word "give up" in the verse (NIV), or "yielded up the ghost" (Syriac version), but commentary explains that "'yielded up the ghost,' or 'dismissed the Spirit', means that He sent it away, and gave it as a free offering and sacrifice as proof of His love. (Schofield, 1917). Based on this lesson and commentary I have read, it is my interpretation, that when you choose to forgive someone, you aren't *giving up anything*. You aren't forfeiting anything. You **are** allowing yourself to claim the peace that God's love provides with the act of yielding up your pain and hurt. Personally, I would much rather live with peace.

Faith

Faith isn't just "belief," it isn't something *you have*, it something that *God gives you....*

Ephesians 2:8 (NIV) - "For by grace you have been saved through faith and that not of yourselves; it is the gift of God."

True faith is based on an unfaltering and sincere trust in the Lord that also comes from learning His Word, something that you will do the rest of your life, and by studying and learning, your faith *will* grow...

Romans 10:17 (NIV) – "So then faith comes by hearing and hearing by the Word of God."

And it doesn't take a lot...

Matthew 17:20 (NIV) - "So Jesus said to them, "Because of your unbelief; for assuredly, I say to you, if you have faith as a mustard seed, you will say to this mountain, 'Move from here to there,' and it will move; and nothing will be impossible for you."

I think the most apt biblical description of "Faith" is Hebrews 11:1 (NIV) – "*"Now faith is the substance of things hoped for, the evidence of things not seen."* I love this verse, but on any given day if you ask me to tell you the scripture, I draw a complete blank. I am a work in progress, and as smart as God made me, I have the worst time remembering book, chapter, and verse. I think that being able to recall Scripture comes with taking time to study His Word.

In relation to the other elements I have touched on in this chapter, know this; "eternal life is achieved by grace through faith," and "without faith it is impossible to please God." *(1 John 5:4; Heb 11:6).* Put more plainly, you can achieve eternal life by God's gift of unmerited favor to you [grace], through your sincere trust in Him even though you may or may not have any direct physical evidence of His existence [faith].

I think a very important element in building my faith (clarity I got from a Beth Moore bible study), is making sure that I dress, EVERYDAY, in the amour of God described in **Ephesians 6: 14-18 (NIV):**

"14 Stand firm then, with the belt of truth buckled around your waist, with the breastplate of righteousness in place, **15** and with your feet fitted with the readiness that comes from the gospel of peace. **16** In addition to all this, take up the shield of faith, with which you can extinguish all the flaming arrows of the evil one. **17** Take the helmet of salvation and the sword of the Spirit, which is the word of God. **18** And pray in the Spirit on all occasions with all kinds of prayers and requests. With this in mind, be alert and always keep on praying for all the saints."

Each of these elements of protection (belt of truth, breastplate of righteousness, feet fitted in the gospel of peace, shield of faith, helmet of salvation, sword of the spirit) protect us from what Satan might send to destroy us. In my case, those tools Satan used to try to destroy me after the loss of my husband were tools like grief, depression, hopelessness, guilt, worry, and fear. The shield of faith is something that I find particularly important to point out here.

The shield of MY faith is [should be] based on WHO GOD IS, NOT WHAT GOD DOES.

Take a moment and let that settle on your spirit.

When I was doing this study, I hadn't really thought about that. For instance, let's say that I let my faith in God be determined by *my perception* of what God had done for me the day Jonce died. If you had asked me that night or maybe even shortly thereafter, I might very well have said, "He didn't do anything. He didn't save Jonce. He could have and he chose not to, He didn't *do* anything that night. Nada. Zip. Zilch. He Left me completely hanging in the wind."

The reality is, God did many things that night for me and the months leading up to Jonce's death, but I hadn't realized that at the time. If I had chosen to believe that God had somehow abandoned me and hadn't done anything for me, when he actually had, I would have missed many blessings. If I had chosen to believe that God's existence hinged upon whether or not Jonce lived, I think that my faith might, very well, have been obliterated. God, in His infinite wisdom, and for reasons my tiny mind is unable to comprehend, has a plan. He IS the creator. He IS the Alpha and Omega, He IS the final authority.

Just because I don't know His reasons for what He does or does not do, will not change who He IS. Furthermore, my personal experiences are not the basis for the Word of God. Just because I don't feel like my personal experiences on this earth are reflective of God's greater plan, doesn't mean that His greater plan isn't real. Now, I get up everyday, and I know that God has a plan for my life. Do I have clue one what that is? Not yet. I am getting better at listening to Him, so I am starting to feel there are certain things He wants me to do. But definitively, do I know? No. I do not. I just know that if I study the Scriptures, have faith in who HE IS, trust in Him, accept His mercy and grace, believe that He died for me, that He has washed me clean, that I further his Kingdom by serving Him *(James 2:14-17)*, and I live by faith, and not by sight, then He **will** use me for **His** glory, goodness, and purpose.

"And we know that in all things God works for the good of those who love him, who have been called according to his purpose."

Romans 8:28

Peace

Finding peace can be a real booger, but I think I have traveled a long way in the last two years. I don't know if it's because I have family who are in ministry and my foundation as a kid took good root, or if losing Jonce made me more receptive to listen to Him. All I know is that God made me. I am His child. He knows a loss greater than any other does. He *sacrificed* His son for all of mankind. When looking at loss in this perspective, I kind of feel that the losses I suffered through my life really aren't that big of a deal. But *my losses are* a big deal. They are a big deal *to me,* and they are **a big deal to God.**

These are some of the most personally comforting verses I have found in Scripture. I liken the concept of peace as the culmination of all the other elements in this chapter. A person can't achieve peace with a situation or person, *God gives you that peace.* However, I find it more difficult to receive peace from Him if I am lacking in faith of who He is, if I haven't recognized His grace and mercy, or if I deny forgiveness to myself or another person.

John 14:27 (NIV) - "Peace I leave with you; my peace I give you. I do not give to you as the world gives. Do not let your hearts be troubled and do not be afraid."

John 16:33 (NIV) - "I have told you these things, so that in me you may have peace. In this world you will have trouble. But take heart! I have overcome the world."

Psalm 29:11 (NIV) – "The Lord gives strength to his people; the Lord blesses his people with peace."

The antithesis of God's Peace is anguish. The etymology of anguish is "to choke." Anguish can be a part of grieving in which you find yourself feeling like you just got dragged through a keyhole backward. If you don't recognize anguish for what it is, and pray about receiving God's peace, it becomes a simmering toxic cloud that will choke you with anger, suffering, dread, make you writhe in pain *(Psalm 55:1-5)*, anxiety, and mental torment. All one nice big nasty little present from Satan tied up in a big red bow strapped to a stick of dynamite. It will rip you up one side, down the other, and make you wish you were never born.

Anguish is all of those things combined, but it is different from just grief, sadness, depression, or any other singular emotion. It's different, because of the element of mental torment. Anguish destroys not only your mind, it torments your spirit *(Job 7:11, Isaiah 65:14)*. I can't recall exactly the number of times I cried out to God after Jonce passed. Alone in my moments at home, on the porch, or in the car, I would cry out my anguish over my loss because I felt like I had done something to deserve it. I apologized, I lamented, I tried bargaining, and I tried getting results by becoming angry. None of which were fruitful mind you.

However, over time, with healing, praying, becoming involved in church, finding friends who understood my loss, and surrendering to God, I found my anguish birthed new gifts from God. Most predominately, those have been peace and joy. Anguish doesn't have to remain in your life.

Anguish can co-exist with joy…

2 Corinthians 7:4-7 (NIV) – "**4** I have great confidence in you; I take great pride in you. I am greatly encouraged; in all our troubles my joy knows no bounds. **5** For when we came into Macedonia, this body of ours had no rest, but we were harassed at every turn-- conflicts on the outside, fears within. **6** But God, who comforts the downcast, comforted us by the coming of Titus, **7** and not only by his coming but also by the comfort you had given him. He told us about your longing for me, your deep sorrow, your ardent concern for me, so that my joy was greater than ever."

Grief and joy can trade places and anguish can *turn into* [birth] joy….

John 16:20-22 (NIV) - "**20** I tell you the truth, you will weep and mourn while the world rejoices. You will grieve, but your grief will turn to joy **21** A woman giving birth to a child has pain because her time has come; but when her baby is born she forgets the anguish because of her joy that a child is born into the world. **22** So with you: Now is your time of grief, but I will see you again and you will rejoice, and no one will take away your joy."

One thing I guess I hadn't realized until lately is that God is tenderhearted to our pain, and he feels our loss. In the bible story of Lazarus, we see Jesus's capacity for pain and suffering in compassion for His people. The short recap of the story is that Jesus hears of Lazarus's death, and arrives four days after Lazarus has passed away to comfort Lazarus's sisters Mary and Martha. Jesus had reasons why He waited in coming until Lazarus had been dead four days.

John 11:20-40 – 20 (NIV) - When Martha heard that Jesus was coming, she went out to meet him, but Mary stayed at home. **21** "Lord," Martha said to Jesus, "if you had been here, my brother would not have died. **22** But I know that even now God will give you whatever you ask." **23** Jesus said to her, "Your brother will rise again." **24** Martha answered, "I know he will rise again in the resurrection at the last day." **25** Jesus said to her, "I am the resurrection and the life. He who believes in me will live, even though he dies; **26** and whoever lives and believes in me will never die. Do you believe this?" **27** "Yes, Lord," she told him, "I believe that you are the Christ, the Son of God, who was to come into the world." **28** And after she had said this, she went back and called her sister Mary aside. "The Teacher is here," she said, "and is asking for you." **29** When Mary heard this, she got up quickly and went to him. **30** Now Jesus had not yet entered the village, but was still at the place where Martha had met him. **31** When the Jews who had been with Mary in the house, comforting her, noticed how quickly she got up and went out, they followed her, supposing she was going to the tomb to mourn there. **32** When Mary reached the place where Jesus was and saw him, she fell at his feet and said, "Lord, if you had been here, my brother would not have died." **33** *When Jesus saw her weeping, and the Jews who had come along with her also weeping, he was deeply moved in spirit and troubled.* **34** "Where have you laid him?" he asked "Come and see, Lord," they replied. **35** *Jesus wept.* **36** Then the Jews said, "See how he loved him!" **37** But some of them said, "Could not he who opened the eyes of the blind man have kept this man from dying?"

Jesus Raises Lazarus From the Dead

38 *Jesus, once more deeply moved*, came to the tomb. It was a cave with a stone laid across the entrance. **39** "Take away the stone," he said. "But, Lord," said Martha, the sister of the dead man, "by this time there is a bad odor, for he has been there four days." **40** Then Jesus said, "Did I not tell you that if you believed, you would see the glory of God?"

More than once (see passages in bold italics), it is clear that Jesus was deeply moved by the grief of Mary, Martha, and the people of the village that had come to comfort the sisters. Earlier in verse *John 11:5*, it states that Jesus loved Martha, Mary, and Lazarus. He understood Mary and Martha's loss, and was pained Himself at the loss of someone He considered a friend. Verse 35 is the shortest sentence in the bible, and in my opinion, the most powerfully descriptive of how God mourns with us and feels the pain that we feel.

Actually, I have two viewpoints on this particular verse and I am sure it has been debated among scholars at some point. On the one hand, I feel that "Jesus wept" because Lazarus had died. He missed His friend, but He was also weeping in compassion for the sisters and friends who also loved Lazarus. On the other hand, I wonder if He wept, in part at least, because He knew that He would raise Lazarus from the dead. Did He weep because He knew that Lazarus was with the Father and Jesus knew that He would rip him away from Heaven to bring Lazarus back to this earthly existence?

In the months following Jonce's death, I spoke about spirituality to several people, asked questions, cried, and asked more questions. Then I attended church, and had this discussion about Lazarus with Ronny and a couple other people. In the end, I think Jesus wept for a combination of both of the reasons above, not just one. I believe that Jesus loved Lazarus and wanted His friend back, but He also understood what raising Lazarus actually meant. Let's face it, Jesus, above all others, knew what it meant to be present with the Father, and all of the peace and heavenly glory this would have included. I think it is entirely possible He wept because He knew what He was taking Lazarus away from by bringing him back to life.

❦❦

In the days and months following Jonce's death, I wished him back, I begged, I cried, I pleaded, I offered to swap places. I had no shame. I just wanted him back, no matter the cost. The thing that stopped me from doing that was the realization of what I would be pulling him away from. *How much did I really love Jonce?* Did I love him enough to trust God that He knew what He was actually doing? Did I love Jonce enough to let him go, and let him go willingly from my heart into the heart of God? Did I want him so badly to satisfy my own hurt, that I would literally keep asking to rip him away from his creator? No. I was not willing to keep asking God to sacrifice Jonce's eternal peace to satisfy my own wants or needs. I realized in order for me to really be at peace with what had happened, I needed to wholly surrender myself to God's authority, even if I didn't understand the situations I had been placed in, or God's decisions, actions, or my perception of His lack of action.

I wish I could adequately convey the feeling of unadulterated comfort and peace that surrender to God gives you. There is no other comparable human experience. As inadequate as this is, let me try to paint a picture for the reader. Picture a time when you were little. Picture a time when you were hurt or sad, and the **only** thing that made you feel better was your daddy. You are crushed, hurt (physically or emotionally), and torn in half. You climb into your daddy's lap, curl up in a small ball, stuff your head down against his chest, and sob. You cry until your tears won't come, and you possibly even fall asleep. The whole time, your daddy rubs your back, strokes your hair, and whispers that everything will be OK. Soft rubs, low whispers, a gentle rocking. As I said, it is a completely inadequate description, but it's the best I have to offer.

In my anguish grief, and despair after losing my husband, I would have sworn I would never be happy again, and I would never know true joy again. All of that died when Jonce did. In that pain, I crawled up into my Father's lap. He whispered that He had a plan for me even if I didn't understand. He rubbed my back, stroked my hair, gently kissed the top of my head, and told me that He *understood* my pain and my loss, and that He was sorry I was hurting. He also assured me that everything was going to be OK, even if I couldn't see that just yet.

13

THE GOOD LIFE…

I have referenced Beth Moore in this book a few times. She is not the only bible study author I have studied, but I find her the most compelling and the one who teaches in a way that speaks most clearly to my heart. Part of her study of the book of *James* focuses on *James 3:13-18*.

Earlier in the book, I told you what I wanted after Jonce died:

- I wanted to be happy.
- I didn't want to be sad anymore.
- I didn't want to feel guilty for things that happened or didn't happen.
- I wanted unabashed forgiveness for the way I had wandered.
- I didn't want to feel miserable for things I couldn't change.
- I didn't want to feel accountable or beholden to anyone out of a feeling of obligation.
- I wanted to be a better person.
- I wanted to feel something more/bigger than me.
- I did NOT want to go through this again if I could help it.
- I wanted to feel comforted and unconditionally loved again.

Now, in the scope of *James 3:13-18*, what do these things mean exactly? I wanted to start a new chapter in my life. I wanted a good life. In this passage of the study on James, we were watching the accompanying DVD for the study. In that session, Beth Moore asked her students to answer the question, "What is the Good Life?" Naturally, I started writing down what I thought this meant while she was talking. I wrote down:

- Peace
- Happiness with what I am blessed with without being demanding or self-absorbed
- A strong family
- To make enough money to pay bills, but not so much if it would corrupt me
- To make enough money to be able to give back to others or help others in need

That was as far as I got in my list before I got a little tap on the shoulder. I turned back to the television. She starts in on the list of what "The Good Life" entails. [Tip: Always watch, listen, **and then** write your answers]. A couple of my answers could have been wedged into this list, but not all of them. I was looking at the immediacy of my earthly situation, not the immediacy of my spiritual situation. The list of elements that make "The Good Life" are:

- ❖ A life that saves us from ourselves (2 Timothy 3:1-5) NIV
- ❖ A life that has a track record of yielding to others
- ❖ A life that is full of Mercy (John 10:10) NIV
- ❖ A life that is full of good fruit (John 15:16) NIV

James 3:13-18 - "13 Who is wise and understanding among you? By his good life let him show his works in the meekness of wisdom. 14 But if you have bitter jealously and selfish ambition in your hearts, do not boast and be false to the truth. 15 This wisdom is not such as comes down from above, but is earthly, unspiritual, devilish. 16 For where jealousy and selfish ambition exist, there will be disorder and every vile practice. 17 But the wisdom from above is first pure, then peaceable, gentle, open to reason, full of mercy and good fruits, without uncertainty or insincerity. 18 And the harvest of righteousness is sown in peace by those who make peace."

So. What did this set of verses mean in relation to having "The Good Life?" For me, this set of verses from James means that the things and trials of this world would often feel insurmountable. We are not meant to be here, but while we are here, we need to watch out and be mindful of several things as children of God:

- Knowing how to cope with the pressures and trials the world throws at us is true wisdom, and we are not wise on our own, that comes from God.
- We are NOT defined by your circumstance of this world.
- Meekness does not mean weakness. Greek for meekness is *praotes* or *prautes (noun); praos* or *praus (adj.)*. To have the quality of meekness means that one has great power under control.
- We should conduct our lives and affairs in a self-forgetful manner and be wary of the things of this world such as self-ambition, jealousy, and greed because those things will give us a false identity in who we really are (God's child) and pull us under into the things of this world.
- Worldly wisdom does not provide peace. It is poison, and worldly wisdom will bring us down, get us to a place where we feel trapped, and then beat us about the head and ears with evils of this world.
- Wisdom that comes from ambition or jealousy is not of God. It is of the world, and that kind of wisdom promotes our own advancement at the expense of others.
- Wisdom from God is "pure, then peaceable, gentle, open to reason, full of mercy and good fruits, without uncertainty or insincerity." This means if the wisdom is boastful, self-serving, or at the expense of someone else, we seriously need to reevaluate what kind of wisdom it is we are being given. I *promise* you, that kind of wisdom if not from God.
- God's wisdom will bear good fruit in your life, a strengthening and/ or restoration.
- Good fruits of this world (at least in my world) are peace with God and peace with others in my life. Being a servant to not only God, but also my friends, family, and community.

Let me put this a little more bluntly and in "laymen's" terms: Keep your eyes and ears on God, and look for wisdom that gives you a sense of peace and understanding. If you are getting a sense of unease, jealousy, greed, hatred, etc... in your "wisdom" then rest assured that's not God. That's Satan and the world pulling your strings. Speak lovingly, be sweet, do good works, and be the hands and feet of God so that the world can bear witness to your good fruit. Don't boast, and don't place yourselves in a position of getting ahead in this world by chopping everyone else off at the knees. It's not Godly, and frankly, it's just not nice.

The study on James is so in-depth and there is so much to gain from just this single epistle in the Bible. Of course, I find that to be true about my study on David, and Kelly Minter's study on Ruth. As a suggestion to my readers, I highly suggest getting into one, even if you feel a little lost, or just even if you aren't sure that, you *want* to do a bible study. Being receptive to God's word takes practice. Sometimes I feel obtuse at times, and I get frustrated when I feel like we don't understand His Word. Even so, I think it is important for me to learn His word so that I can understand Him better.

Bible studies are wonderful in eliminating the feelings of "I feel like a moron," "I can't follow this," "I am never going to understand all of this," "the bible is just too overwhelming and complicated." Bible studies take things in manageable chunks and get you moving in one direction, and ultimately make you hungry to learn more. Currently I feel like someone who hasn't eaten a decent meal in years and just got turned loose at the all-you-can-eat buffet at Ryan's.

I am happy to report that the "Good Life" that I long for, is in the works. I am studying the Word, giving, and being a servant to others and to God, building new relationships with God, my new family, my church, and others in my community. I think that as I practice finding wisdom through his peace, that my orchard will produce bountiful harvests of good fruit. My life circumstances won't always be puppies and rainbows. I'm sure I will see floods, heavy snows, and the occasional drought as I trudge through the world, but God's wisdom to weather the storms is easy to hear if I just listen for it.

14

$\mathcal{M}$y GOOD LIFE…

THANK YOU, JESUS!

Since Jonce's death, I am building my relationship with God and the people in my life in a more profound way. I am a changed person. I don't have to justify myself or how I feel about God to anyone in my life. I am not the same "me" that I was a little over two years ago. I have more clarity of mind, and I have my eyes focused on The One Most Important in my life. I try to study The Word (ineptly most of the time, but that's why we have bible studies and fabulous teachers and friends). I also try to put my hands and feet into action with church or in other areas, that I feel God leads me to help.

Don't get me wrong, I am far from where I hope to be one day. I know God is still working on me, and I know I will, by my very human and fallible nature, have periods that leave much to be desired. However, I want my new husband and my stepchildren (past and present) to be able to see in me that I am a changed soul, that I am hungry for God, and that He has complete authority over my life, and no one else. I stumble, I fall, I screw up, and I am forever asking for forgiveness and restoration. I am completely, totally, and utterly imperfect.

I am human, thus I sometimes feel that I am not good enough, that I am too rough around the edges, that I am a disappointment to Him and others, and that I am constantly failing when I study His Word. I always feel like I am "missing something." I have wonderful news for you… that's part of being human, and part of having to live in this world. I will spend the rest of my earthly life learning His Word, and I am never going to have time to learn all of it, so I am going to learn and practice what I can before He calls me home.

With feelings of self-doubt and inadequacy in the forefront of my mind, I made several conscience decisions:

- First, I AM wonderfully and unequivocally a huge mess. God and I **_LOVE_** my mess, so there.

- Secondly, we don't belong here, and life is just going to completely disappoint us and hurt us sometimes. People die, friends get cancer, car accidents happen, etc…There is no way around it, so I just have to roll with it, pick myself up, and get after it again and again.

- Thirdly, I am going to sin, as is my human nature. However, I will seek Him out, study his Word, ask for discernment and forgiveness, and make myself accountable to what I have learned.

- Lastly, and most importantly, I think I have learned that God doesn't want me to be anybody but me. He made me; He knew my "Bridgette design" from the beginning. It's not like any of this is a shocker to Him. He knows my flaws, my fears, my everything. His engineering was perfect. Granted, the operator error ratio is really high, but if it's good enough for Him, it's good enough for me.

Having come to these conclusions, I feel completely comfortable saying that if someone doesn't like me, doesn't like my journey, or wants to judge me for who I am, where I have been in my life, where I am now, or where I am going…well….then have at it. I know who I was, who I am, and I am learning who God wants me to be. In short, I can't please everyone all the time and the only one I really should be worried about pleasing is God.

⋞⋟

Life is not a fairy tale, obviously, so I am almost hesitant to conclude this book in a manner that some may find "hokey." However, I think ending on the good points in my life is important, because the whole point of the book was to demonstrate through my testimony, that life gets better. Life moves forward, and it can become something amazing, even in the face of a tragic and seemingly insurmountable loss. I wouldn't have ever thought that in two years from Jonce's death, I would be able to say I love my life and that I am happy. Praise God that I can, because He *is* the reason that I am.

Ronny is an amazing husband. He is a Godly man, he takes very seriously his role as spiritual leader in our home, and he is a supportive and loving man. He has supported the foundation I created in Jonce's memory, my writing this book, my educational goals, and he is the most kind and loving person I think I have ever known. I was blessed with him in mammoth proportions. Not that He needs my accolades, but "Great Job, God!"

Ronny and I married on the beach in Gulf Shores, Alabama with several guests and about 300 onlookers. I highly suggest getting married in a public venue. The thunderous applause from hundreds of onlookers was something I think everyone should experience. It was most touching to me because I felt like it wasn't just the onlookers applauding; it was as if God provided an extra element of glee. It sounded like a touchdown cheer at Bryant-Denny Stadium, something I am sure Jonce would have wanted for me. To that, Ronny and I both give a hearty, "Roll Tide!"

My two stepdaughters are amazing as well. One is a junior at Judson College, and the other a freshman at the local high school. Both are quick-witted, sweet, respectful, kind, tenderhearted, and extremely bright. Any stepparent would be blessed to have these two young women in their life. They know that I truly love their dad, and that I consider them my own.

I have completed my doctoral program and I am waiting with great anticipation to participate in the commencement ceremony. I completed this arduous journey and I am humbled, excited, and completely petrified (in a good way) of what comes next. God's driving this car. He doesn't need my backseat driving. He will tell me what to do with the degree, and He will open the doors to what comes next. I just wait for Godwink confirmations of what He needs me to do.

The Hubble Foundation has been established in memory of

Jonce and is up and running. Not full steam yet, but it is starting to gain speed. It's an organization to promote safety for tower workers, scholarships for children of fallen tower dogs, and an advocate organization for change to industry safety regulations. It's a marathon, not a sprint. We have a long way to go, but we have already awarded two scholarships! Finding these children is more difficult than I thought, but God will open a path for me to find them (www.hubblefoundation.org).

I don't have a tremendous amount of contact with Jonce's family, but overall I think that is to be expected. The boys are older and have their own life. I hear from Becky occasionally, and she appears to be doing well. I need to make more of an effort to connect with her, but I don't want her to think I am "creeping" or trying to interfere in her life. I speak to Jason and B.J. regularly, and they have helped with a fundraiser for Hubble Foundation. Other family members and I have contact, but it's infrequent. I think that's part me and part them, but overall, I feel that everyone in Jonce's family is adjusting to a new normal, as best they can, me included.

` I love each and every person in Jonce's family. I want them to have peace, joy, and happiness in spite the loss we have all suffered. Some family members may find what they are seeking for a while, and some will find peace a little sooner. All I know to do is to use the most powerful tool in my arsenal, prayer.

God has enabled me to be able to work part time. Currently, I am a professor with the University of Phoenix, and President of my own non-profit. Running the Hubble Foundation, teaching part time, being active in the church, helping others fundraise for various causes, and being a wife and mother again is more than full time work for now.

I remember getting antsy the other day because I am not working a "clock-in / clock-out" 40-hour job right now. Then I remembered I specifically had asked for that. I asked God after Jonce died to enable me to be able to take the time off from a full time job to focus on these things listed above. He gave me that and I am forever grateful. The fact I was getting nervous or concerned about the job situation just goes to show that humans are forever meticulous, needful creatures that are rarely satisfied with anything. We are truly an exasperating creation. Where God gets his patience befuddles me. I asked, I received, and then caught myself getting all ramped up over it. To calm my fears, I had an internal conversation/realization from the

Holy Spirit (indulge my imagery; it works best in my head):

> ***God sitting in a chair, slightly bent over, looking down at me, thumb and forefinger pinching the bridge of His nose...Deep Sigh, with a tiny bit of exasperation and a smile***

"Child, I hear from you *a lot*. Don't get me wrong, I **love** that, but sweetie, did you not ask for the time to get all of this done?"

"Uh, yes Sir. I did, didn't I?"

sheepish grin from me

"What is it that you are worried about?"

"Umm, OK, we'll see, now I realized, I asked and I received. I guess I need to kind of finish what I've got going before getting all worked up, huh?

He smiles

"That's kinda the idea, yes. And for the record, you don't have to get all worked up."

"I know that, I really do! I just was going to say that I know I will have to work full-time again, and I guess I was just a little worried that..."

He smiles and slightly shakes his head and belly laughs

"Uuuuhhh, *giggle* never mind. I keep forgetting that You got this already in the works huh?"

"Yes sweetie, something like that."

"Alrighty then, I am done being a pest, I'm good."

"No, you are MY child. You are beautiful and amazing, and you are ***never*** being a pest. Now, don't you have some work to get done? Grading papers, running a foundation...."

"Yes Sir, I know I seem to say it a lot but, Sorry, Thank you and I love you!"

"It's ok, you're welcome, and I love you."

I think to close the book following this little display of imagery; I will share with you the most amazing realization I have had in the last two years. The realization was slow building and kind of abstract for quite a while. I am a firm believer that you can hear something repeatedly, and sometimes it just doesn't click. Then one day...BAM! DING DING DING DING DING!!! This is one of those things.

It came to me in a video bible study. That Bible I was holding in my hand, everything in that Bible, every parable, every promise and covenant, every word of comfort, wisdom, love…every last syllable, that's **_mine_**. It was written *for me*, it was written *about me*, it was written *to me*, it was written *to hold me, comfort me, and teach me*.

It might have been written eons ago, but it was written for me. *The same way it was written for you.* It's not some abstract collection of parables and stories to amuse your fancy. It is life's instructions to you from your Maker, it's your offensive weapon against Satan, and it's your tether no matter the storm. I have heard people complain that God is not tangible, that they don't have physical proof of Him. Really? Seriously? I have several copies of tangibility in my home and one in my car (usually).

Not only is the Word the tangible, physical representation of God, it smells sweet, it moves, breathes, changes, and reveals new things every single time that you explore His promises and His breath contained in its pages.

<***I am excited…I know I am on the right track writing this. I took a break, went on the porch, got Godwinked, and was mauled by a black and blue butterfly***>

God will guide you and teach you every time you sit with Him or when you read and study with someone (or a group) in your life. Close your eyes, hold His Word, breathe deep, and let it take you over. Those profound moments when you can feel Him and hear Him have no discernable pattern to them, but when He gets into you, there is no earthly expression to tell you how it feels.

I am so humbled that you took the time to read my story. It's no more special or mundane than anyone else's journey. It's just mine. I don't expect to rock worlds or change lives. I just wanted to express how my journey has and continues to change me. As I have repeatedly said, I am a work in progress and will be until my last breath. I am also sure of one thing no matter what. Ronny and I say it aloud together every day. God Loves Me.

Love,
Bridgette

Jarhead Rides Blade in Tribute

Graveside. Hardest Day of My Life *Courtesy of Wanda Williams,
Raw Images

Ronny and I on our wedding day 7/28/2012 *Courtesy of Wanda Williams, Raw Images

Haley, Lauren, Ronny, and me *Courtesy of Wanda Williams, Raw Images

$\mathcal{L}$OST, HURTING, & TIRED?

I tried to write this book so that my personality came through while not whitewashing my pain. In the same way, I am not going to whitewash anything else. We all get tired, feel hurt, and get overwhelmed. We all reach a breaking point where it seems like we are alone and can't take the struggle anymore. If you are there, and you want the real relief that only God can give, then I invite you to read this prayer (either to yourself or with someone). By reading the prayer in earnest, and being completely open and truthful with God when you pray this, you can start your life anew in Him.

You do not have to confess the prayer in front of a large group of people in church, and you do not have to be baptized. Being baptized, in my opinion, is important. John the Baptist baptized Jesus. It represents symbolically becoming a new creation in Christ, so I will not ever minimize its importance. However, baptism is not a requirement for your salvation. You are saved through His grace, not by being submersed in water. When you choose to hand your life over to Christ, you are born a new creature:

2 Corinthians 5:17: "Therefore if anyone is in Christ, he is a new creature; the old things passed away; behold, new things have come."

2 Corinthians 3:18: "But we all, with unveiled face, beholding as in a mirror the glory of the Lord, are being transformed into the same image from glory to glory, just as from the Lord, the Spirit."

Dear Lord,

I am so tired. I have not been where You would have me to be. I have not been the person I know that You have created me to be. I want to rest in Your peace, mercy, and love. I have strayed away from

You, and I am sorry for the ways I have disappointed You. Lord, I am asking You to change me. I am so weary, and you promised us that You would give us rest if only we came and asked You. I am asking You now. Please, Lord, come into my heart, and make me a new creature in You. Guide me and create me into the person You would have me to be. I ask You Lord to come in my heart and give me salvation. I believe that you sent Your only begotten son, that He perished on the cross for my sins, and that He conquered the grave and rose again.

In Jesus Name, Amen

APPENDICES

Worship Music For The Soul

Britt Nicole	All This Time
Building 429	Listen to the Sound
Building 429	Where I Belong
Chris Tomlin	All My Fountains
Jason Gray	Remind Me
Jeremy Camp	Overcome
Kelly Minter	You Called My Name
Kutless	Carry Me to the Cross
MercyMe	The Hurt and the Healer
Sidewalk Prophets	Live Like That
MercyMe	You Are I AM
Francesca Battistelli	The Stuff You Use
Matthew West	Forgiveness

*I hear more songs every day that I think, ohohohohohohoh!!! that's me, that's me!!! Worship music can invade your soul and give you expression when you can't find your own words. I have been singing a song in the house and dropped to my knees in the middle of cleaning because the Holy Spirit moved in on me. Even if you have never really listened to worship music before, I encourage you to do so. It can be very healing and soul cleansing.

GODWINKED:

Precious Butterfly Stories I Received after Jonce Passed

These are direct cut and pastes from Facebook pages. My friends often refer to me as "Gette" (pronounced "Jet," a nickname derived from my first name.

Pamela

I remember a ride soon after, I never saw so many at one time in my life. I was all over the road trying to miss them, smiling the whole time thinking of u both. Still think of u 2 when I see one…and remember our ride to gulf shores…memories, what would life be like without them…hugs

Erik

Not long after, I was in my yard, and a single, solitary butterfly seemed to follow me around the back yard. It would land somewhere when I stopped, but when I started moving again, it took off and stayed in my vicinity. Couldn't help but think of you.

Ali (Alison Sloan)

Just wanted to know that I was thinking about you. Yesterday was a bad day for me. I missed my turn off the interstate and I realized was headed to the McCord office. Well …you know I tried to talk myself out of it but something just pulled me right on in. I got to see the guys but I didn't stay long because it had me so upset. I also saw two butterflies on the way home Thursday circling each other and I thought of Jonce and Barry. Have fun love u

Heather (My BFF)

When Jonce told me he was going to ask you to marry him, I asked him one simple request. Please love her and take care of her she is most precious to me.....having said this I now want to thank all the Alabama family, because that is what you guys are, for being there for Gette when she needs family and friends the most. I'm sorry for not being there as I would like to be, but Gette know that I love you and Jonce did keep his promise. You are loved.

Shawn I just heard about Jonce this morning. I read your UPDATE so I will dispense with all the mushy stuff and tell you something you already know. Jonce made people he touched a better person. I can HONESTLY remember on a few occasions thinking that I wish I could have his character. Jonce was the kind of guy that after not seeing me since 2005 would have picked up the conversation right where we left off and we would have had a great time.

It was my HONOR to orchestrate that night on the stage in Memphis.

I know after I left the south I was bad at staying in touch with everyone. Life sort of got in the way but let's both try to do better.

Wanda

Just so you know... there were butterflies all around us today at the range with gunny. I know Jonce was just sneakin' in there trying to spend a little gunny time. Made me smile. love you!

Haley Coe Hester

August 17, 2010

When I was packing my car Saturday to come to school a small light yellow butterfly flew into my car around all my stuff in the car and then flew away, it was all very quick... I thought of you. :) love you!

Kim

hope you are doing well. I just wanted you to know we went camping this weekend and were surrounded by butterflies!! It was hard not to think of Jonce. Rick and I got teary eyed. Keep your chin up girl - lots of love your way!

Peggy

Every butterfly I see reminds me of Jonce. We were on the boat Wednesday and one kept landing on my foot. :) We love you Bridgette!

Kelly

Just went to Rinse My Car off. And, when I was walking to the car. Lo and, Behold there was a Butterfly on the Car, on the back windshield and, Rear.... Where all my Alabama stuff, is... It would fly and, land, fly and, land... 1st one, I have seen, all Summer Long... I Believe, I just got a Visit... Made me, Cry.... Maybe he was letting me know he heard my prayer for butterflies.... Wouldn't that just be the most awesome thing in the world?.... Gosh, I am speechless, Gette.... I never experienced anything, so real.... Love You....

Please visit and share the Hubble Foundation, Taking Climber Safety to New Heights, at www.hubblefoundation.org.

Your support is immensely appreciated!

Hubble Foundation is a 501(C)3 Corporation

Made in the USA
Coppell, TX
01 February 2021